MORE MERRYTHOUGHT MAGIC

The bears, pandas and koalas

Pat Rush

Merrythought

Copyright © 2003 by Pat Rush

First published in the UK in 2003

ISBN 0 9545392 0 6

Printed by Livesey Ltd., Shrewsbury

Published by

Merrythought Limited

Dale End, Ironbridge, Telford, Shropshire

Contents

INTRODUCTION

There cannot be many more satisfying projects in life than the publication of a book such as this one describing such a world famous English family manufacturing company.

It therefore gives me, as Managing Director and Grandson of the founder, much pleasure in bringing this book to our collectors and followers worldwide.

Our authoress, the highly talented Pat Rush, has spent literally years compiling, originating and writing this much needed work which quite justly makes a wonderful sequel to the original first book on Merrythought Limited *The Magic of Merrythought* written by John Axe in 1976.

The quite countless amount of pleasure which Merrythought products have brought to the world population over the 70 plus years of production must be an overwhelming figure.

Our rarer Merrythought antique pieces are now commanding ever increasing values at auction and the existence of this book will give more providence to our products both old and not so old in this beautifully presented volume.

We therefore invite you to turn the pages and explore the stunning variety of unique and innovative Merrythought designs both old and new. We very much hope that this book gives as much pleasure to the reader as it has to ourselves.

Oliver Holmes

FOREWORD

Merrythought has produced countless bears during its long history. A book of this size could not possibly hope to describe, let alone picture, them all. In any case, details of many have been lost, and in other instances all that remains is an old catalogue picture.

I have used as many photographs as space permits, and have tried to include brief descriptions of other bears, where possible, in the hope that these, too, can help collectors to identify examples not illustrated. In this way, I have been able to include something, however brief, about virtually every bear, panda and koala that has appeared in a Merrythought catalogue - and many others that have not.

I have added a comprehensive index, to make it easier to track down the relevant information - and to follow the history of a bear, from its introduction to its disappearance from the range. But readers may also find it helpful to refer to the earlier volume about the company - *The Magic of Merrythought*, by John Axe - which includes charts giving dates and sizes of items included in the catalogues.

Pat Rush, December 2002

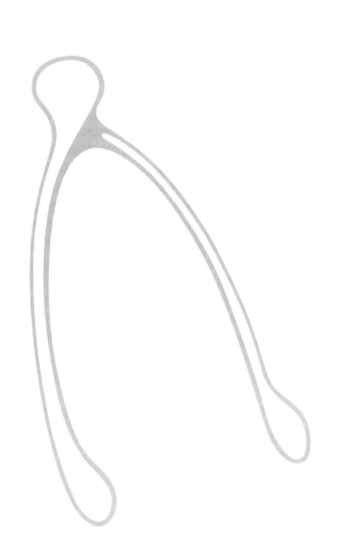

Chapter 1

1. THE MERRYTHOUGHT STORY

On 10 September 1930 a new company was registered - its objectives being "To manufacture and deal in toys, games, amusements, dolls, playthings and fancy goods of all kinds in plush, felt, velvet, wool, fur, skin, cotton, metal, celluloid, wood, rubber, card, paper or any other material etc." Its first directors were given as H.C. Janisch, a West London toy manufacturer, and C.J. Rendle, a toy manufacturer from Wellington, Shropshire.

The company was Merrythought Ltd. Nearly three-quarters of a century later, it is still making a huge variety of high-quality soft toys - although its objectives have also been widened to include the creation of numerous limited editions aimed at the adult collector.

The business was set up in Coalbrookdale in Shropshire, but its roots were actually further north in Yorkshire, where W.G. Holmes and his partner G.H. Laxton had set up a spinning mill back in 1919. They imported raw mohair from such countries as Turkey and South Africa, and spun it into mohair yarn, which they then sold to various weavers of mohair cloth - among them the firm of Dyson Hall & Co. Ltd, in Huddersfield.

Mohair cloth was used in many different ways - for seat coverings, carpets and rugs as well as coats, suits and other items of clothing. It was widely employed in seating for theatres and cinemas, for example, but by the 1930s demand was declining as other materials came into favour. Dyson Hall was one of many companies that faced difficult times as a result of this, and eventually Holmes and Laxton bought them out.

The only man in this 1930s picture is C.J. Rendle, one of the first directors of the company.

Large numbers of bears were produced from the outset, as this 1930s picture shows.

Their sales director knew C.J. Rendle, who was head of toy production at Chad Valley in Wellington, Shropshire. It was also known that he was unhappy there, so when Holmes and Laxton decided to set up a soft toy company of their own (a useful outlet for their mohair), they knew exactly who would be the right person to put in charge of it. Rendle moved the eight miles from Wellington to Coalbrookdale, bringing with him a number of other Chad Valley employees.

One was the designer Florence Atwood. Rendle's daughter Mavis was unable to hear or speak following a bout of meningitis, and attended a special school in Manchester. Florence was one of the older girls there, having lost her hearing in a childhood accident. When she left the school, Rendle found work for her at Chad Valley (where she specialized in the designing of soft toy animals), and she moved with him when he left.

Rendle's fellow director in the new business, H.C. Janisch, had been head of sales for another major soft toy manufacturer – J.K. Farnell, based in West London. He was placed in charge of sales for the new venture, and was based in its London showroom – situated in Holborn Circus (113 Holborn). He and his wife lived in a flat there as well, along with their son Duncan, and he travelled up to the factory just once a week.

In the factory, much of the work was carried out by hand, although there were benches of power-driven sewing machines – initially operated by a large light-oil engine, but this was soon replaced by electric motors. There were 12 or 14 machinists on each of the two benches, with a driving shaft that ran the whole bench. So if the belt on one machine broke, the whole bench had to be switched off so that it could be replaced. These days there are individual machines, which solved this problem.

The factory in the 1930s.

A machine was used to cut out the felt pads, and machines were also used to cut out the discs for the joints, but most of the work – from stuffing to finishing – was carried out by hand. The firm even made up its own boxes, which were bought flat and then machined together. The whole production of the toys was thus very labour-intensive.

Initially, 20 workers were employed by the company, but that number soon grew as orders began to flood in. By the end of January 1931, the firm was already receiving excellent reviews for the "splendid range of high-class soft toys" that it had exhibited during its first trade show. A month later, it was reported that orders were exceeding even "the most optimistic anticipation".

As the number of employees needed to cope with them increased, it soon became clear that Merrythought's initial, temporary accommodation would not be enough to house them all. Within months the company was moved into former foundry buildings on the banks of the River Severn, just half a mile away from the famous structure that gives the town of Ironbridge its name. Merrythought is still in the same place today, although the factory has grown considerably since those early days. At one time it employed around 200 workers in all, although the advent of such aids as stuffing machines have reduced the number needed today.

Bears were included in the firm's very first catalogue, and have been in production ever since. But they always accounted for just a part of Merrythought's extensive range of soft toys, which has also included every imaginable kind of animal, not to mention the dolls. New designs were introduced every year, right from the start, and invariably some would be more in demand than others. The bears were always popular, however, and the only time that production of them virtually ground to a halt was during the Second World War.

With the outbreak of war, the Merrythought factory, like most of those making soft toys in Britain, soon turned to the production of more essential items. The factory itself was used for map making, amongst other things, but some machinists were moved to the Norah Wellings factory in Wellington, and a stuffer and two finishers were kept on at Ironbridge.

Among the toys they made at this time were dolls produced from cloth fents, or short ends. But when war was imminent Rendle had decided that it would be a good idea to secure some government contracts for the factory. As a result, Merrythought soon began turning out such items as bags for gas masks and leather linings for steel helmets, as well as chevrons for uniforms and first-aid armlets. They were all things that involved cutting and machining – processes that were also a part of soft-toy making – but the machining was done in Wellington during the war years.

Buildings in use in the 1930s still form part of the factory today.

When production of toys resumed, around 1946, materials were in short supply, and the firm's recovery was further hampered when the River Severn burst its banks, destroying much of Merrythought's work-in-progress as well as many of the old samples. By 1947, however, production was once again in full swing – with

Bears are again in evidence in this late 1930s photo.

the firm initially concentrating mainly on items for export, as Britain attempted to rebuild its economy after the hostilities.

The factory was by then being run by Leo Hirst - the son-in-law of Dyson (from Dyson & Hall), who had previously taken over the running of the London sales office (which moved to Moorgate in 1937). Then, in 1948, Trayton Holmes - son of founder W.G. Holmes - joined the business, and set about turning it into a more profitable concern.

He met Jim Matthews of Dean's, who agreed to market the Merrythought toys as well as those by Dean's - and Matthews' connections with the major London department stores, such as Selfridges, and with Disney brought new orders for Merrythought. The firm would go on to make many toys under licence to Disney, including Winnie-the-Pooh and his friends.

Most of the other toys at this time were created by Jean Barber, who had replaced Florence Atwood (who died in 1949). She remained at Merrythought until the

mid-1960s and was followed by a whole succession of other designers until Jacqueline Revitt joined the company in 1972. Apart from a period of illness, Jacqueline has been designing the majority of the Merrythought toys - and more recently collectors' items - ever since.

Changes instigated by Trayton Holmes included the introduction of more modern sewing machines, and also of stuffing machines. He had learned that these were being employed by factories in the USA, and commissioned the mechanics at the garage opposite the factory to create two for him.

In the early 1970s, his son Oliver - then in his early 20s - also joined the company, after training initially as an engineer. He eventually succeeded his father as Managing Director and he, too, brought about changes both to the factory itself (once renowned for being both cold and dirty) and to the production process.

He remembers how, when he arrived, most of the cutting out was still done by hand, using templates and ink to draw the pieces on to the back of the cloth. Machines were generally only used to cut out the pads and the velveteen toys. Today, presses are much more widely used.

The years have also seen many changes in the bears and other items produced, with Merrythought always quick to make use of the latest fabrics and the latest techniques. Not least has been the advent of many bears (and some other items, such as dolls and gollies) made specifically with collectors in mind – many of them in limited editions.

The following chapters will attempt to give an overview of many of the bears (and also the pandas and koalas) that have appeared during the decades that have elapsed since the founding of the company. However, with such a vast number of different creations over the years, there is no way that the coverage of them can be anywhere near complete.

In the late 1930s, pandas were very much in demand.

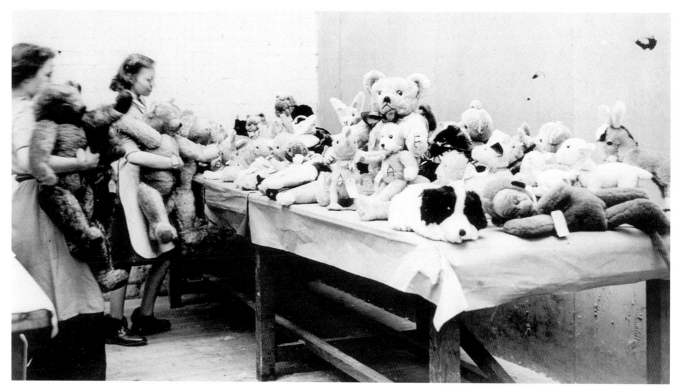

Samples being prepared for the British Industries Fair in the late 1930s or the early post-war years.

Two of the women seen in this 1950s picture are still working for Merrythought today.

Chapter 2

2. THE 1930s

Right from the start, bears were an important part of the Merrythought range. But although large quantities were sold, the number of different designs was initially small. There were just four in the company's first catalogue, dated 1931. Two were traditional, fully jointed bears - one of which was destined to become a real classic.

This 24 inch (61cm) bear in the Merrythought archives is thought to be one of the first made by the company, and to date from around 1931. Unusually, his identifying button is on the back of his ear, which may have been turned round at some stage.

Today he is widely known as the Magnet. But closer inspection of the early catalogues suggests that this name may originally have been intended for another design - referred to as a "really cheap line", and available in gold and various other colours. There were four sizes in all, ranging from 12.5 to 24 inches (31.5 to 61cm), and the three largest were fitted with "automatic growl".

Pictured alongside him was the chunkier Merrythought Bear. The mohair version, available in either gold or the latest "Sunkiss" shade, was said to be

"feather-light and beautifully finished" and was made in no fewer than ten sizes, ranging from 13 to 26 inches (33 to 66cm). The two smallest were fitted with squeakers, while all other sizes had "best quality squeeze growls".

There was an art silk version as well, costing slightly more and said to be of the same quality and finish. These were available in the first eight sizes (up to 21 inches or 53.5cm), and there were also eight colours in all - Salmon, Ciel, Myosotis, Iris, Canary, Crimson, Copper-glow and Jade - said to be the "1931 selections of the Paris Dress designers". In the 1930s, as now, not all soft toys were made for children. In certain circles they were at that time also a highly desirable fashion accessory.

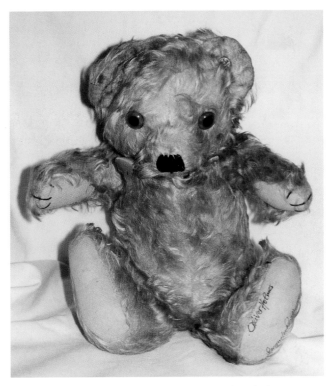

This Bingie Sitting Cub, made from a tipped mohair, measures around 11 inches (28cm) and the Merrythought button in his ear confirms that he dates from the 1930s. He also has a label on the inside of his left leg. The signatures on the footpad were added much more recently.

That said, there is no doubt that the majority were bought for the young and the very young, and the two Merrythought bear cubs introduced in 1931 were clearly created with these age groups in mind. Best-known today is the sitting Bingie, originally made in a tipped brown and white curly plush, with white ear linings. Said to be "cuddley and winsome", he had a jointed head and arms, and was on sale in three sizes – 9, 11 and 14 inches (23, 28 and 35.5 cm).

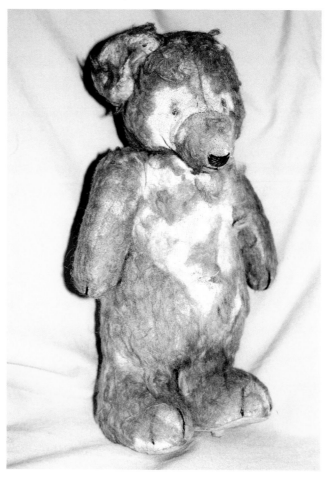

The baby bear known as Tumpy was on sale for just two years, from 1931, and is today extremely rare. The woolly plush of this one was originally blue, and he has jointed head and arms.

The Bingie Sitting Cubs, as they became known, would remain in production for many years. But the standing Tumpy, first seen at the same time, was less enduring. Although the catalogue referred to him as the "baby ... that appeals, appeals, and appeals!", he had disappeared from the range within a couple of years. Made from a soft woolly plush in "dainty colours", with a white chest and tum, white muzzle and white ear linings, he too was made in three sizes, this time 12, 14.5 and 17 inches (30.5, 37 and 43cm).

In 1932, the number of pages in the catalogue doubled, but again bears were featured on just a handful.

The Bingie cub and Tumpy were still there, however. Both were apparently unchanged from those of the previous year, except that the Bingie was now available in three additional sizes – 16 inches (40.5cm), 19 inches (48cm) and one simply described as "a good show piece". (The following year the size was given as 26 inches, or 66cm.)

The original Magnet, on the other hand, had disappeared, but the range of higher-quality Merrythought Bears had been expanded considerably. For a start, there was a new 12 inch (30.5cm) size. There were also now three different mohair versions, namely one in light gold, one (slightly more expensive) in old gold, and a brand-new "best quality" version in a long-piled curly mohair that was said to be "a real aristocrat among bears". All 11 sizes were also now available in art silk, but there were new colours for the new year. Eglantine, Azur, Nil, Copper, Red, Gold, Mimosa, Venus and Clematis were, according to the catalogue, the 1932 selections of the Paris dress designers.

The Cutie Bingie, first seen in 1932, was one of the first toys to have the articulated "Movie" joints in the lower limbs. He was made in three sizes.

There was a new Baby Bingie too – a sitting cub, like his bigger brother, but this time in assorted colours of art silk. Included in a range of light and soft Teenie Toys, intended for small babies, he was made in 5.25 and 7 inch sizes (13.5 and 18cm). In addition, a Cutie Bingie was one of the new Movie Toys, which had a special kind of articulated joint in the lower limbs, enabling them to be posed in all sorts of different positions. He was made in 10, 12.5 and 15 inch sizes (25.5, 31.5 and 38cm).

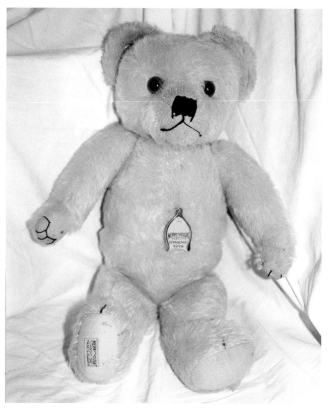

The button just visible in the right ear of this 19 inch (48cm) ted helps to pinpoint his date to the 1930s; it is exceptionally rare to find a bear from that time still wearing his original swing tag.

Another new design was a Laughing Baby Bear, said to be a "new conception of a 'toy' bear cub". The catalogue pointed out his "natural shape" and the fact that he could either stand upright or sit in a chair. But his most striking feature was his open mouth. Available in three sizes – 12.5, 15 and 18 inches (31.5, 38 and 45.5cm) – he was made from art silk in two different colourways, namely golden brown with biscuit and black with white. Presumably the contrasting colours referred to the pads and possibly the mouth lining, although this cannot be seen clearly in the catalogue illustration.

Some early Merrythought bears – especially smaller ones like this – had identifying buttons on their backs. The eyes here are replacements, and the nose has been restitched.

There were toys based on real bears as well, including Polar Bear Cubs on all fours in the Movie Toys range. "All these toys have movable joints," notes the catalogue, "and can be made to sit, stand or beg, and take up many other positions." Also new was a Baby Polar Bear called Sammy. He is pictured in a sitting position but, as he is fitted with collar and lead, he could presumably also stand on all fours.

A wheeled Brown Bear was on all fours as well – described as a riding model and produced in five sizes ranging from 17 to 38 inches in length (43 to 96.5cm). Riding Polar Bears were available too. An internal steel frame provided the necessary strength, and the animals were mounted on a steel chassis with "Ackermann steering". The four larger sizes were also fitted with pull growls.

New, too, was a toy described as a Bush Baby, but which was said to be "modelled on the Australian tree bear". The Merrythought Trials Book, in which the designer described new toys in varying degrees of detail, confirms that this was, in fact, a koala. He was available in art silk - either grey or colours - in four sizes, ranging from 7 to 14 inches (18 to 35.5cm).

The following year saw few changes to existing lines. Tumpy had disappeared from the range, however, and there were also fewer varieties of the popular Merrythought Bear, although a new 30 inch (76cm) size had been added. He was no longer offered in art silk, and the number of mohair versions had been reduced to two - the original light gold and a new "best quality" series in "curly piled mohair plush".

The dressed bears in the Bingie Family were first seen in 1933. This version was the boy Bingie, and his costume was described as a "Pickwick" suit. He measures 20 inches (51cm).

That same year (1933), tiny "Bingie" bears were also turned into cot toys and rattles, fitted with rings and bells. But the most notable new arrivals of the year were the Bingie Family, dressed in a variety of outfits. Only the heads and hands were made of mohair. Underneath the

clothes, the bodies were made of cloth (referred to as canvas in the Trials Book), and they had a new slim shape to show the garments at their best.

At 27 inches (68.5cm), the Grenadier was taller than his fellow Bingies, on account of his black busby, but the bear himself was identical to others in the series, with head and paws made from mohair. Bear courtesy Bears Everywhere.

A number of different versions were available, including a Sailor Bingie in sailor suit, white sailor hat and black tie. The suits could be dark blue, light blue or white, and the bears were made in 15 and 20 inch sizes (38 and 51cm). Then there was the Grenadier, with his scarlet tunic and black busby, trousers and shoes. He, too, was made in two sizes, but the height of the busby meant that the final measurements were 20 and 27 inches (51 and 68.5cm).

There were boy and girl Bingies as well, he wearing a two-coloured "Pickwick" suit and she a pretty dress made of satin or organdie. In each case there was a choice of colour combinations. Also on offer was a "Ski-Girl"

1934–5

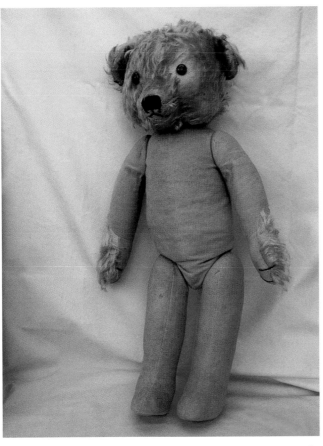

Mohair was used only for the visible parts of the Bingie Bears. Under their costumes, their bodies were made from cloth.

The Merrythought Trials Book, which details all new designs, mentions a "cheap" blue and pink bear in 1934. It is possible that this fully jointed ted, with his short-pile mohair, may have been one of them.

dressed for winter sports in a knitted jumper and cap, with velveteen trousers and felt shoes.

A year or two later, a Highlander was added to the range – dressed in full regalia, with red tunic and tartan kilt, white tartan-trimmed spats, black shoes, and tartan-trimmed black tam-o'shanter. Today, however, it is rare indeed to find any member of the Bingie Family still in his original clothes. Sadly, these were often removed during play and subsequently lost, so that examples still wearing their original outfits are now highly prized by collectors.

The Merrythought catalogue for 1934 and most of that for 1935 are unfortunately missing from the Merrythought archives, so fewer details are known of the ranges for those years. But the Trials Book mentions a "cheap" blue and pink teddy, created in 1934, while a 1935 Price List includes the first Dutch-style Teddy Bear and a photo of him has luckily been preserved. It can be seen that only his head and paws were made of plush.

This Dutch-style Teddy Bear apparently appeared in the 1935 Merrythought catalogue, and is slimmer than the two 1938 designs. The body was the same as that used for some Dutch dolls.

His body and arms were in the form of a cloth shirt, while his legs were wide Dutch-style trousers. Longer and leaner than the later Dutch Bear and Dutch Teddy, he was made in 15 and 18 inch sizes (38 and 45.5cm).

Bobby Bruin, first seen in 1935, was designed to be more like a real bear than a teddy, and had special "Movie" joints, so that his legs could be moved into any position.

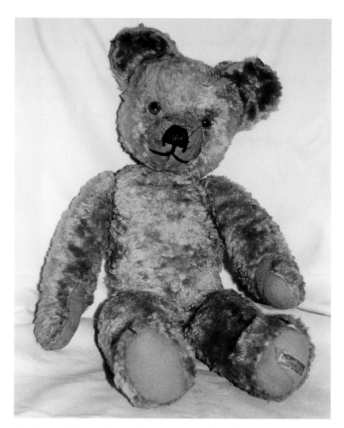

Early art silk bears in traditional colours, like this one, are especially rare. He measures 16 inches (40.5cm) and is believed to date from the mid 1930s.

Also included in the 1935 list was an alpaca version of the Bingie, and a Bobby Bruin with the now patented "Movie" joints. Designed to be more like a real bear than the traditional teddy, his legs could be moved into any position, so that he could sit, stand or "walk". Made from mohair, he was available in 17.5, 20.5 and 26 inch sizes (44.5, 52 and 66cm).

Noteworthy, however, is the number of classic teddy bears on offer that year. In addition to that once known as the Merrythought Bear, it appears that there was now a new variation, as well as further versions of the design originally known as the Magnet. All again appeared in 1936.

In contrast to the 1931 catalogue, however, in 1936 it was the style once labelled the Merrythought Bear which was now described as the budget line. Made from gold mohair with a medium length pile it was "produced expressly for the cheap market". The old Magnet Bear, on the other hand – once a "really cheap line" – was now being made in two qualities. The art silk version was available in seven different shades and with a very soft kapok filling. Also described as "very soft stuffed" was a bear in "short close pile old gold lustrous plush", said to represent "the finest Teddy made".

Alongside them was a new fully jointed bear, offered in two different kinds of long-pile mohair – one gold and shaggy and the other biscuit brown tipped with a deeper shade. Distinctive claw stitching (rather like large blanket stitches) is clearly visible in the catalogue photo. It would become a feature of many Merrythought bears from the 1930s and beyond. Also visible is the characteristic nose, with extra long stitches at either side extending downwards (although often only slightly).

Soft stuffed and enormously appealing, it is these bears which are today often referred to as Magnets – the "bears that attract" – and they are keenly sought by collectors. In particular demand are those that have a celluloid-covered metal button inserted into one of their ears or, in the case of smaller bears, sometimes on the back of the body. The buttons carry the Merrythought name along with the wishbone logo, and were used in addition to the usual foot labels.

The specially jointed Bobby Bruin was still on sale in 1936 as well. So too was the Bingie sitting cub, now in five sizes – 9 to 18 inches (23 to 45.5cm) – and in a "warm brown colour, long pile plush". The dressed Bingie Sailor, Guardsman and Highlander were likewise featured once more, although the Boy and Girl (still listed in 1935) had now disappeared. The 7 inch (18cm) Baby Bingie, on the other hand, had been converted into a toy for the youngest baby by the addition of elastic and a bone ring.

Long, silky mohair was used for many bears made before the Second World War, and a button in the ear confirms the date of this example, which has the familiar "webbed" claws of those today generally known as the Magnet bears.

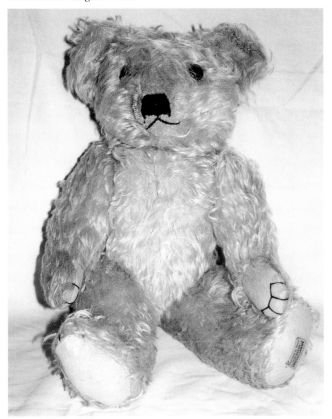

The Chubby Bear, made from brown alpaca, was available in four sizes. This one, at 9 inches (23cm), was the smallest and is in almost pristine condition in spite of his age.

The only new teddy that year was the endearing Chubby Bear in brown alpaca, with fawn muzzle and feet. He was available in four sizes, ranging from 9 to 20 inches (23 to 51cm), but his extreme rarity today suggests that relatively few were sold.

By the following year, he had disappeared from the catalogue, although the Bingie cub, the Baby Bingie cot toy and the three dressed Bingies were still there, and the classic jointed teds also remained unchanged.

New, on the other hand, was the highly distinctive Teddy Doofings – the most posable Merrythought toy thus far. Not only did his arms move, for instance, but also his fingers and, as the catalogue picture implies, even his mouth and eyes could be made to open and shut. He was shown in a variety of different positions, and an accompanying verse also made one or two exaggerated claims:

> He can laugh, he can cry
> He can sing, he can sigh
> He can sweep, he can sleep
> He can box and darn socks
> He can play any way.

Virtually every part of Teddy Doofings could be made to move - even his mouth and eyes. Today, he is one of the rarest of all the Merrythought novelties. Photos Leanda Harwood.

The first of the Merrythought pandas arrived in 1937, and they were made in especially large numbers in the months leading up to the Second World War. The nose stitching is typical of pandas made at that time.

He was a fairly large bear, measuring 22 inches (56cm), and available in brown, blue, pink or green (with brown apparently the most popular). Today, in any colour, he is among the rarest of all the Merrythought novelties.

The same year was also notable for the arrival of the very first Merrythought pandas. There were two designs, one of them really just a black and white teddy and listed as a "Panda" Teddy Bear. Made in five sizes (14 to 25 inches, 35.5 to 63.5cm), his arms, legs and the top of his

An "eminent scientist" supplied Merrythought with details on the appearance of real pandas, and this example on all fours was the result. He first appeared in the late 1930s.

1937–8

body were black. So too were his ears, and there were black patches under his eyes. But there was no attempt to reproduce the shape of the real animal which was, said the catalogue, a rare species, with no living specimen in any zoo.

Also in the catalogue, however, was a much more realistic Panda Bear on all fours, said to have been modelled from data supplied by an eminent scientist. He was available in two sizes – 8.5 inches (21.5cm) high/17 inches (43cm) long, and 11 inches (28cm) high/21 inches (53.5cm) long.

This Bingie Sitting Cub is made from mohair, but he is very similar to one in alpaca pictured in the Merrythought archives and dating from around 1937.

There was a wheeled Riding "Panda" Bear on all fours as well, measuring 18 inches (45.5cm) high and 20 inches (51cm) long, while a Riding Grizzly Bear was offered in three sizes, ranging in height from 18 to 31.5 inches (45.5 to 80cm).

Very different again was the new Bombardier Bruin, made from art silk. Available in five sizes (12 to 24 inches, 30.5 to 61cm), he included a special "Stayput" fitting, which enabled him to sit more naturally.

Made from colourful art silk, Bombardier Bruin had a special fitting, so that he could be made to sit naturally even though he had no joints.

By 1938, the Riding Panda had disappeared from the catalogue, but the rest of the range had been retained and there were now two new "Dutch" style designs. The Dutch Teddies had heads, arms, bodies and feet made of soft alpaca, while their legs were in the form of wide Dutch-style trousers, made from corduroy. On the front of the trousers were two felt pockets, and the bears were designed to stand with their paws tucked into these.

There were eight sizes in all, the smallest just 7 inches (18cm) in height and the largest a giant 26.5 inches

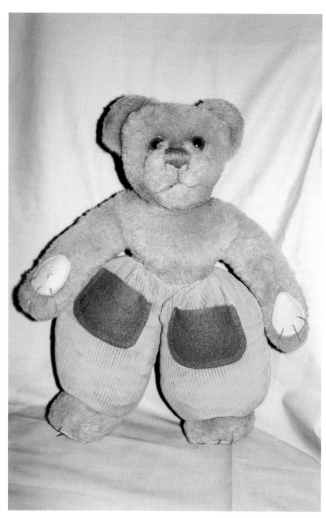

Alpaca was used for the head, body, arms and feet of the 1938 Dutch Teddy, while wide Dutch-boy trousers made from corduroy formed his legs. The catalogue listed eight sizes in all.

The Dutch Bears, illustrated in the 1938 catalogue, had mohair heads, while their bodies and limbs were in the form of sewn-in clothes that included wide, Dutch-boy trousers.

(67.5cm). According to the catalogue they were fitted with growls, but most of those that have turned up for sale in recent years have had no voice box – although one or two have been complete with squeaker.

The Dutch *Bears* were likewise designed to stand with their paws in the pockets attached to the front of their trousers. In their case, however, only the head was made of plush, and it was mohair rather than alpaca. Body, arms, legs and feet were of cloth – again with the legs taking the form of wide Dutch-boy trousers. There were three sizes – 11.5, 16 and 21 inches (29, 40.5 and 53.5cm).

The Merrythought archives contain no 1939 catalogue, and it is possible that the 1938 range remained on sale into the following year. But a 1939

supplement detailed many new designs, including various bears.

The "soft and light" Kiddies Kuddle Kubs (also called Kiddies Kuddly Cubs) included three bears, for instance. The smallest, Bobby the Bear, was just 8 inches (20.5cm) tall and made from alpaca plush, with a soft moulded head. Then there were the 9 inch (23cm) Teddie and the 10 inch (25.5cm) Baby Bruin. Both were soft, fully jointed, and again made from alpaca, with Teddie in fawn and Baby Bruin in shell pink.

The same catalogue also introduced a new variant – in burnished bronze mohair – of the traditional jointed bear with Merrythought's distinctive paw stitching. But a look through the company's Trials Book for the early months of 1939 shows a preoccupation with another

The pads on the front paws of this bear have been replaced, making it impossible to see the original stitching, but he still has his original felt foot pads. He is believed to date from the late 1930s, but could be a little later.

soft toy, namely the panda. The arrival of a baby panda called Ming at London Zoo had captured the public's imagination in the gloomy months when war was looming, and Merrythought was quick to respond, as the supplementary catalogue testified.

Three smaller sizes of the teddy-style Panda Bear – 9, 10 and 12 inches (23, 25.5 and 30.5cm) – were added to the existing five ranging from 14 to 25 inches (35.5 to 63.5cm), and there were totally new designs as well. Little art silk mascot panda teddies measuring just 5.5 and 7.5 inches (14 and 19cm) were designed to be carried around by all ages. There was an unjointed Cuddly Panda Doll, measuring 11.5 inches (29cm) and said to be ideal as a slumber toy. A 9 inch (23cm) glove

puppet enabled the owner to "imitate the Panda's amusing antics", and the sitting Chummy Panda was a more lifelike version. With jointed arms and head, and with realistic-looking stitched claws, he was made in five sizes ranging from 9 to 18 inches (23 to 45.5cm).

Other new panda designs included small cot toys and a "Begging Panda" in a sitting position, as well as realistic versions on all fours. The latter were among those that went on sale at the zoo itself, and proved to be in great demand with all the visitors who flocked there for a glimpse of the new arrival.

By early September, however, everything would change. With war imminent, Ming was evacuated to the comparative safety of Whipsnade and just two days later war was declared. Before long it would bring virtually all Merrythought toy production to a standstill.

During the 1930s, art silk bears were made in a wide variety of colours and sizes. This blue example measures 15 inches (38cm) and has the "webbed" claw stitching seen on many 1930s Merrythoughts.

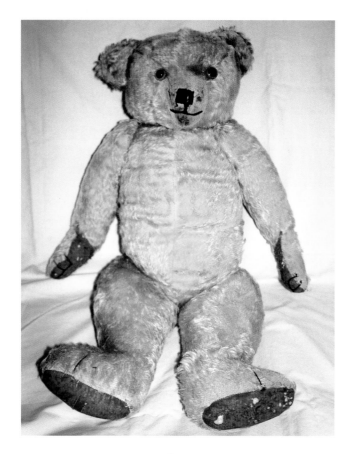

LEFT: *The plush used for this large (26 inches/66cm) bear suggests that he was probably made in the late 1930s, although similar bears were produced in other mohairs after the war.*

BELOW: *The bear on the left was originally known as the Merrythought Bear. The same illustration was later used for the "H" quality. That in the centre was described as the Magnet Bear in the 1931 catalogue. This illustration was also used for the later "AS" and "AX" Bears. The picture on the right was used for the later "M", "T" and B.B. Bears.*

``H.''            `` AS '' and `` AX.''   "M" and "T."

A button in the left ear of this 16 inch (40.5cm) bear indicates that he was made in the 1930s, when the range included examples in many different colours (not all mentioned in the catalogues). In this case, the original bright red mohair has been bleached by the sun.

Traditional Merrythought Bears

1931
Merrythought Bear
Gold or "Sunkiss" mohair in sizes 13, 14, 15, 16, 17, 18, 19, 21, 24 and 26 inches (33, 35.5, 38, 40.5, 43, 45.5, 48, 53.5, 61 and 66cm)

Art silk – Salmon, Ciel, Myosotis, Iris, Canary, Crimson, Copper-glow and Jade – in sizes 13, 14, 15, 16, 17, 18, 19 and 21 inches (33, 35.5, 38, 40.5, 43, 45.5, 48 and 53.5cm)

Magnet Bear
Gold or colours in sizes 12.5, 15.5, 19.5 and 24 inches (31.5, 39.5, 49.5 and 61cm)

1932
Merrythought Bear
Light Gold and Old Gold mohair in sizes 12, 13, 14, 15, 16, 17, 18, 19, 21, 24 and 26 inches (30.5, 33, 35.5, 38, 40.5, 43, 45.5, 48, 53.5, 61 and 66cm)

"Best quality" in long curly piled mohair, sizes 12, 13, 14, 15, 16, 17, 18, 19, 21, 24 and 26 inches (30.5, 33, 35.5, 38, 40.5, 43, 45.5, 48, 53.5, 61 and 66cm)

Art silk – Eglantine, Azur, Nil, Copper, Red, Gold, Mimosa, Venus and Clematis – in sizes 12, 13, 14, 15, 16, 17, 18, 19, 21, 24 and 26 inches (30.5, 33, 35.5, 38, 40.5, 43, 45.5, 48, 53.5, 61 and 66cm)

1933
Merrythought Bear
Light Gold mohair in sizes 12, 13, 14, 15, 16, 17, 18, 19, 21, 24, 26 and 30 inches (30.5, 33, 35.5, 38, 40.5, 43, 45.5, 48, 53.5, 61, 66 and 76cm)

"Best quality" in curly piled mohair, sizes 12, 13, 14, 15, 16, 17, 18, 19, 21, 24, 26 and 30 inches (30.5, 33, 35.5, 38, 40.5, 43, 45.5, 48, 53.5, 61, 66 and 76cm)

1934, 1935
No catalogues in Merrythought archives, but 1935 Price List includes "AS", "AX" and "T" Bears in the same sizes as in 1936. An "H" Bear is also listed in the same sizes as in 1936, with an additional 25 inch (63.5cm) version.

1936, 1937, 1938
"H" quality
Medium length pile gold mohair in sizes 12, 15.5, 17 and 21 inches (30.5, 39, 43 and 53cm)

"AS" Bear
Art silk bears in seven different shades (not specified in catalogues) in sizes 12, 13, 14, 15, 16, 17 and 18 inches (30.5, 33, 35.5, 38, 40.5, 43 and 45.5cm)

"AX" Bear
Short close pile old gold "lustrous" plush in sizes 10.5, 12, 13, 14, 15, 16, 17, 18, 19, 21, 24 and 26 inches (26.5, 30.5, 33, 35.5, 38, 40.5, 43, 45.5, 48, 53.5, 61 and 66cm)

"M" Bear
Rich gold long pile shaggy mohair in sizes 12, 13, 14, 15, 16, 17, 18, 19, 21, 24, 26 and 30 inches (30.5, 33, 35.5, 38, 40.5, 43, 45.5, 48, 53.5, 61, 66 and 76cm)

"T" Bear
"Medium novelty quality" long pile mohair in "biscuit brown ground colour, tipped with a deeper shade", in sizes 14, 16, 18, 21 and 26 inches (35.5, 40.5, 45.5, 53 and 66cm)

1939
B.B. Range in burnished bronze mohair, in sizes 12, 13, 14, 15, 16, 17, 18, 19, 21, 24 and 26 inches (30.5, 33, 35.5, 38, 40.5, 43, 45.5, 48, 53.5, 61 and 66cm)

Chapter 3

3. THE 1940s–50s

1940–2

As with most soft toy companies, the Second World War brought many changes to Merrythought as the factory gradually turned to the making of more essential items. No further soft toy catalogues appear to have been published until 1947, although new toy designs continued to be described in the Trials Book up until 1942. They even included a few bears.

The date of this small bear (approximately 9 inches/23cm in height) is uncertain; it may have been made just before the Second World War, or shortly afterwards.

In late December 1939, for instance, prototypes for two new dressed Bingies were made. One was dressed in a W.A.T.S. (Women's Auxiliary Territorial Service) uniform, consisting of skirt, hat and coat, while there was a new sailor's outfit as well, including trousers, jersey and hat. A few days later, in early January, another was dressed as a soldier. Whether any of these actually went into production, however, is not known.

Towards the end of 1940, a cot toy was designed in the form of a sitting teddy. There was also a "standing teddy bear", said to have his "hind quarters lower than shoulders", but again it is not known whether these actually went on sale.

By 1941, new designs had become very few and far between, but the Trials Book details a total of ten, of

which two were teddy bears. One was described as a "standing bear" with head the same as a teddy bear. Presumably this was a bear on all fours, as the length from his nose to his hindquarters was given as 14 inches (35.5cm).

Also noted, however, was a design for a child's respirator case, to which a toy made of American cloth and plush had been attached. The bag itself was made of gabardine. No description of the toy was given, but later in the year another design for a respirator case specified that a 12 inch (30.5cm) teddy with trousers made from American cloth had been attached. Sadly, no illustrations have so far been found, and again it is not known whether these designs ever went on sale. So although one or two gas mask holders decorated with Merrythought-like bears have turned up in recent years, it has not been possible to identify their manufacturer with any certainty.

In 1942, the number of new toy designs entered in the book was down to a mere five, only one of which was a

Very few bears appeared during the war years, but Merrythought records suggest that this bell boy was designed in 1942. His head, paws and feet are cotton plush, while his costume is made from blue felt and red velveteen.

bear. With shortages of materials by then acute, plush was used only for his head, hands and feet. The body and limbs were made up like that of a golly, using a print fabric.

No more teddy designs would be recorded for more than four years. In fact, the Trials Book shows no new toy designs of any description for the whole of 1943, 1944

Tummykins was one of the first new bears to be designed after the war, and was available in various colours, with contrasting muzzle and ear linings. His legs are "hinged" on to his body.

and 1945, and for the first five months of 1946. Of the five entered between June and December 1946, however, one was a new bear called Tummykins.

Made in assorted colours from long-pile plush, he had tummy, muzzle and inner ears made from contrasting fabric, and white plush patches behind his eyes. His head appears to have been jointed, but his arms and legs were "hinged", enabling him to sit easily. There were three sizes, ranging from 12.5 to 16.5 inches (31.5 to 42cm).

Tummykins was pictured in what appears to have been a special export catalogue (dated 1948), along with a Print Teddy clearly designed to make the best use of

This fully jointed mohair bear, measuring 16 inches (40.5cm) was made soon after the war ended, in the late 1940s or early 1950s.

available materials. Only his head was made of mohair plush. His body and limbs were created out of heavy duty print fabrics, which were easier to come by than plush. Interestingly, the catalogue claimed that the 12.5 inch (31.5cm) bear was fully jointed, but the illustration suggested that was not the case – a fact which has been confirmed by the various examples that have come to light over the years. The fitted squeakers mentioned in the catalogue also appear to have been omitted from the version that went on sale.

The same catalogue again featured the classic jointed ted from the 1930s, with his "blanket stitch" claws. He was referred to as the "M" Series De-luxe Teddy Bear, and this time his mohair was described as amber in colour and long. He was fitted with a squeeze growler, and offered in a total of four sizes: 14, 16, 18 and 21 inches (35.5, 40.5, 45.5 and 53.5cm).

Only the head of the late 1940s Print Teddy was in mohair. Various heavy duty print fabrics were used to make the bodies and limbs, since mohair was still in short supply.

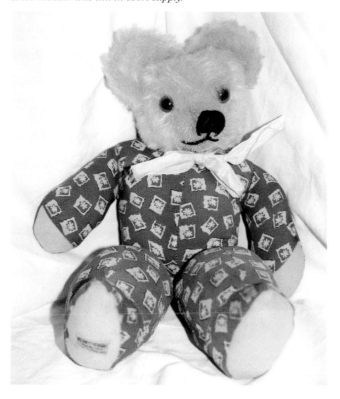

The "H" series bear from the 1947 catalogue; the "M" series bear was the same as that seen in the 1930s.

There was another jointed ted in the same catalogue – in a short-pile golden plush and with more conventional claw stitching. He was described simply as the "H" series bear, available in a total of three sizes, ranging from 15 to 21 inches (38 to 53.5cm). The Bingie was back as well, in a "warm brown colour, long pile plush", in two sizes given as 11.25 and 14.25 inches (or 28.5 and 36cm). Then there was a 7 inch (18cm) Cradle Bingie in "baby shades plush", and the Panda Glove Toy first seen in 1939 had also been reintroduced.

Another early post-war catalogue, dated 1947, also showed the "M" series and "H" series bears – although the sizes of the former were in this case given as 13, 15 and 17 inches (33, 38 and 43 cm) and those for the latter ranged from 12 to 17 inches (30.5 to 43cm). The Panda Teddy, so popular in the months before war broke out,

At first, many of the post-war bears were similar to those produced in the 1930s; only the quality of the mohair enables them to be differentiated.

This rare nightdress case – made in the style of the bear today generally known as the Magnet – did not appear in the Merrythought catalogues, but is believed to date from the immediate post-war years.

The sparseness of the mohair used for this traditional teddy suggests that he was made in the years immediately following the Second World War, although the design is similar to that of pre-war bears.

was included as well, but in just two sizes, namely 10 and 14 inches (25.5 and 35.5cm). The Cradle Bingie was also still shown.

No further new bears were recorded in the Trials Book until January 1949, when the first Merrythought Punkinhead was created (see chapter *Cheeky little bear*). Even in 1950, most of the bears included in the catalogue were pre-war designs like the Bingie cub, the Cradle Bingie and the Panda Glove Toy. The newer Tummykins was still there as well. So, too, were the "M" and "H" series classic jointed bears – but the illustrations for these had changed. Both were shown with longer, upward curving arms than those made in the late 1930s and the 1940s. The legs were more shapely, with plump thighs, and the ears appeared to be much more pronounced.

The "blanket stitch" claws were still there on the "M" series, however, which was offered in four sizes ranging

This illustration was used for the "M", "H" and, later, the "L" series bears between 1950 and 1959.

The materials used for this classic Merrythought suggest that he was made in the late 1940s, when production resumed once more. He still has the familiar "webbed" claw stitching, first seen in the 1930s.

from 14 to 21 inches (35.5 to 53.5cm). That year, though, the same stitching was pictured on the "H" series bears as well, which were made in three sizes ranging from 15 to 21 inches (38 to 53.5cm). In fact, the only difference between the two series in 1950 appears to have been the mohair used – a rich gold shaggy variety for the "M" series and a medium-pile gold for the "H" bears. All could be fitted with growlers.

The 1951 and 1952 catalogues showed only limited changes to the bears, although a new 30 inch (76cm) version was added to the "M" series in 1951 and a new 12 inch (30.5cm) version to the "H" series in 1952. Those measuring over 17 inches (43cm) could be fitted with "tip growlers" if required.

In 1953, on the other hand, the 14.25 inch (36cm) Bingie cub disappeared along with the Panda Glove Toy, and were followed in 1954 by Tummykins and the 11.25 inch (28.5cm) Bingie cub. On the other hand, a new 7

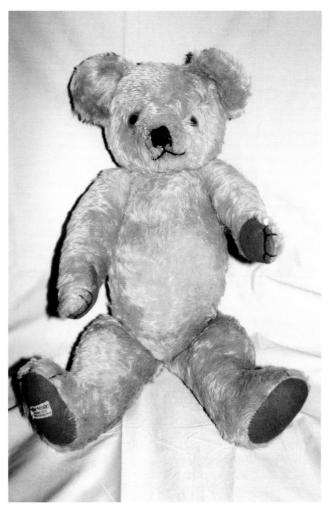

ABOVE: *Bears similar to this one were pictured in catalogues from 1950 onwards, and the label used on the foot helps to confirm that he was made around this time.*

TOP RIGHT: *This unusual little bear has been created from cotton plush and is fully jointed, with a Merrythought label stitched down his back. He dates from around 1950, but did not appear in the catalogue.*

BOTTOM RIGHT: *This 18 inch (45.5cm) ted has an unusually soft filling, and the mohair used to make him suggests he dates from the late 1940s or early 1950s.*

inch (18cm) Cot Bear joined the Cradle Bingie that year, and in 1955 replaced it. The patterns appear to have been identical, but the "baby shades plush" had given way to assorted colours of art silk.

There was also a new 9 inch (23cm) version of the traditional jointed bear in 1954, with the code AS suggesting that this was made of art silk. More extensive changes to the traditional bears followed a year later, however, although the catalogue illustration remained the same. The "M" quality in rich gold shaggy mohair was still offered in the same five sizes as in previous years, but those for the "H" bear in gold medium pile mohair had changed. The 12, 15 and 17 inch sizes (30.5, 38 and 43cm) had been replaced by 11, 13 and 16 inches (28, 33 and 40.6cm). Only the 21 inch (53.5cm) size was unaltered.

In fact, it is possible that the change in sizes resulted from a remodelling of the bear, since the Trials Book includes details of a re-design to reduce the number of pattern pieces. In particular, the body was made up of two pieces only, instead of the more usual four.

A new "L" series was also listed in 1955, made from "best mohair London Gold plush" – a denser pile mohair than the others in use at that time. This version was available in four sizes, ranging from 9 to 15 inches (23 to 38cm).

The only other bear-related item included in that catalogue (apart from the previously mentioned Cot Bear) was an unjointed Panda Bear. The illustration was identical to that of the 1939 Panda Doll, but the sizes had changed to 10.5 and 14 inches (27 and 35.5cm).

All the 1955 bears appeared again in 1956, and that year also saw the arrival of a totally new bear-like creature. Woppit was actually a character in the children's comic *The Robin*, published weekly from March 1953 by Hulton Press – to complement their *Eagle* and *Girl*, which were intended for older children. The tales of Andy Pandy and his Teddy are today the best remembered of the *Robin* stories. But also featured in each issue was "The Story of Woppit", and in 1956 Merrythought introduced a soft toy version of the character. Measuring 9 inches (23cm), his body was made in a "natural 'Woppit' Brown" plush, on top of which he wore a red felt coat and blue felt shoes.

Today he would probably be totally forgotten were it not for the fact that one of the Merrythought soft toys was given to Donald Campbell as a mascot in 1957. Campbell was on the point of attempting a new water-speed record in his hydroplane Bluebird. With Mr Whoppit, as he called him, in the cockpit, he reached more than 239 mph, and from then on the two were inseparable.

They broke many more records together, including one on land of more than 403 mph. Both also survived

Woppit was a bear-like character in a children's comic, but one of the soft toy versions became famous as the mascot of speed ace Donald Campbell.

what was then the fastest automobile crash in history, and when Campbell himself was killed trying yet again to better his time on water, Mr Whoppit again survived. He went on to accompany Campbell's daughter Gina when she twice broke the women's power-boat record.

In spite of all this activity by one of their number, the Woppits did not stay long in the Merrythought range. They were not even included in the 1957 catalogue, which as usual featured just a handful of bears of any description. The "L" series of traditional jointed bears had disappeared too. But the "M" and "H" series remained, along with the old Cradle Bingie (now under the name Cot Bear), and the unjointed Panda Bear.

Totally new, on the other hand, was an unjointed Pastel Bear, made from art silk plush, with white for the head, arms and legs and a choice of pink, blue, red, yellow and dark blue for the body, pads and on the ears. There were bells inside his ears, and he was available in two sizes: 12 inches/30.5cm and 18 inches/45.5cm.

The unjointed Pastel Bear was made from shiny art silk in a choice of shades, and was first seen in 1957.

Also new was a Polar Bear on all fours, made in 9 and 15 inch lengths (23 and 38cm) from white art silk. He, too, had bells in his ears. So did another new 1957 design, the Cheeky, which would go on to become a much-loved Merrythought classic. His story is told in detail in the chapter *Cheeky little bear*.

The Cheeky, the M series and the Cot Bear all appeared in the 1958 catalogue as well, but the Pastel Bear had by then disappeared. His place was taken by a new unjointed bear, which was included in a range of fully washable Jumpee toys. Made from silk plush in assorted pastel colours, the 11 inch (28cm) Jumpee Bears were, like the other Jumpee toys, filled with a special foam stuffing that was not only soft to cuddle but could also withstand a turn in the washing machine. They also had "clamped in" eyes that could not be pulled out by tiny fingers. In the case of the bear, the head was originally based on that of the Cheeky, although it appears to have been modified by the time it went on sale.

Merrythought records suggest that a nightdress case in the form of a panda's head was also introduced in 1958 – although it appears not to have been in any of the regular catalogues. Measuring 12 inches (30cm) in diameter, it had a zipped pocket in the back in which nightwear could be kept during the day. The same design was also available in the form of a cushion, while a smaller 6 inch (15cm) version, known as the Merrycot Panda, was sold as a cot toy. According to the Trials Book, the fabric used was art silk. White elastic with a white ring attached was sewn to the top of the head of the cot toy, and all three versions had bells in their ears.

The Cot Bear – the last remaining Bingie – had finally disappeared by the following year. But the Cheeky was by then established as a regular line, and the "M" series bears, now simply known as Traditional Teddy Bears, remained on offer alongside them. Still made from mohair, fully jointed and kapok-stuffed, the latter were available in the same five sizes as in 1952 and could be fitted with tip growlers. The Jumpee Bear, on the other hand, was now being made in nylon plush, and in just two colours – pastel pink and blue.

This art silk Polar Bear was first seen in 1957 and was available in two sizes.

There was just one new bear-related design that year – a koala made from "Real Australian skin" with foam stuffing. Unjointed, these new toys were produced in four sizes, ranging from 6 to 11 inches (15 to 28cm).

All in all, then, the forties and fifties were relatively quiet years as far as Merrythought bears were concerned. The dawn of a new decade, however, would see them entering the limelight once more.

This bear was designed in 1959 to hold a small hot water bottle inside its body. It is not known whether it ever went into production, but its design is very similar to that of the Chime Bear that appeared two years later.

Traditional Merrythought Bears

1947
"M" series De-Luxe Teddy Bear
Amber colour long plush [mohair] in sizes 13, 15 and 17 inches (33, 38 and 43cm)

"H" series
Golden colour short plush in sizes 12, 15.5 and 17 inches (30.5, 39 and 43cm)

1948 (export?)
"M" series De-Luxe Teddy Bear
Amber colour long plush [mohair] in sizes 14, 16, 18 and 21 inches (35.5, 40.5, 45.5 and 53.5cm)

"H" series
Golden colour short plush in sizes 15, 17 and 21 inches (38, 43 and 53.5cm)

1950
De-Luxe Teddy Bear
"M" quality, made from rich gold shaggy mohair in sizes 14, 16, 18 and 21 inches (35.5, 40.5, 45.5 and 53.5cm)

"H" quality, made from gold medium pile mohair in sizes 15, 17 and 21 inches (38, 43 and 53.5cm)

1951
De-Luxe Teddy Bear
"M" quality, made from rich gold shaggy mohair in sizes 14, 16, 18, 21 and 30 inches (35.5, 40.5, 45.5, 53.5 and 76cm)

"H" quality, made from gold medium pile mohair in sizes 15, 17 and 21 inches (38, 43 and 53.5cm)

1952, 1953
De-Luxe Teddy Bear
"M" quality, made from rich gold shaggy mohair in sizes 14, 16, 18, 21 and 30 inches (35.5, 40.5, 45.5, 53.5 and 76cm)

"H" quality, made from gold medium pile mohair in sizes 12, 15, 17 and 21 inches (30.5, 38, 43 and 53.5cm)

1954
"M" quality, made from rich shaggy mohair in sizes 14, 16, 18, 21 and 30 inches (35.5, 40.5, 45.5, 53.5 and 76cm)

"H" quality, made from medium pile mohair in sizes 12, 15, 17 and 21 inches (30.5, 38, 43 and 53.5cm)

9 inch (23cm) "AS" bear

1955, 1956
"M" quality, made from rich gold shaggy mohair in sizes 14, 16, 18, 21 and 30 inches (35.5, 40.5, 45.5, 53.5 and 76cm)

"H" quality, made from gold medium pile mohair in sizes 11, 13, 16 and 21 inches (28, 33, 40.5 and 53.5cm)

9 inch (23cm) "AS" bear

"L" quality, made from "best mohair London Gold plush" in sizes 9, 11, 13 and 15 inches (23, 28, 33 and 38cm)

1957
Traditional bears
"M" quality, made from rich shaggy mohair in sizes 14, 16, 18, 21 and 30 inches (35.5, 40.5, 45.5, 53.5 and 76cm)

"H" quality, made from medium pile mohair in sizes 11, 13, 16 and 21 inches (28, 33, 40.5 and 53.5cm)

1958
"M" quality in sizes 14, 16, 18, 21 and 30 inches (35.5, 40.5, 45.5, 53.5 and 76cm)

1959
Traditional Teddy Bears
"M" bears, made from pure mohair, in sizes 14, 16, 18, 21 and 30 inches (35.5, 40.5, 45.5, 53.5 and 76cm)

Chapter 4

4. THE 1960s

Since the mid 1950s, Merrythought production had been in full swing once more – no longer affected by the post-war shortages. Each new catalogue invariably featured a variety of new designs alongside old favourites, but bears formed just a small part of the range, and few totally new designs were introduced. That would change in the 1960s, when traditional favourites were joined by more and more novelties, and some well-known characters made under licence.

The 1960 Sooty nightdress case had a zip-fastened sachet in which a child's nightwear could be placed during the day.

Made from a biscuit-coloured mohair, this fully jointed little ted was never included in the catalogue but the fabric suggests that he dates from around 1960.

This Sooty nightdress case was offered in three colours in the Merrythought catalogue, but it is possible that only blue ones actually went on sale.

The first Sooty novelties, for instance, appeared in the 1960 catalogue – both of them in the "Animal Nightdress and Pyjama Case Section". One was all-mohair, based on an enlarged glove-puppet design but with the glove extended to form an almost triangular sachet into which the child's nightwear could be placed. A zip fastener was inserted along the lower edge. The ears and paw pads were black, and a wand was attached to the right paw.

The second design featured a sachet in the form of a velveteen quilted "bed", complete with satin pillow and with a zip fastener on the underside. Attached to the pillow were Sooty's head and paws, in gold mohair with blackened ears – again with a wand in the right paw. The catalogue gives the available sachet colours as red, pink or blue, but a handwritten note on a later catalogue suggests that the Sooty sachet may only have been made in blue.

Another new novelty for 1960 was a Muff Bear, in pink or blue nylon plush. A Cheeky head was attached to a "muff" body, and arms and legs were hinged on to the muff, which was lined with wadding and silk. The foot pads and ear fronts were made from white plush, and a cord attached to the muff enabled it to be hung round a child's neck.

There were more conventional bears too, though, including the Cheekys (which are detailed in a separate chapter) and the Traditional Teddy Bears of the kind first seen in the 1950s. The latter were still available in five sizes, ranging from 14 to 30 inches (35.5 to 76cm), and all but the smallest could now be fitted with music boxes as well as the more usual tip growlers.

The Jumpee Bear in blue or pink nylon was still available as well. So was the Koala Bear made from "Real Australian skin". But these existing favourites had been

Merrythought koalas like this one, made from kangaroo skin, were not actually produced in the Ironbridge factory but were made for Merrythought in Australia.

This small, unjointed Miniature Bear, made from mohair, was introduced in 1960. He measures just 4 inches (10cm) in height.

joined by a totally new design – a Miniature Bear, measuring just 4 inches (10cm) in height. He was a small, unjointed, sitting bear, made from mohair with felt pads and with unusual stitched eyes. Apparently his small size meant that the head had to be sewn on by hand. Initially, he appears to have been made only in a traditional gold mohair, with a suitably short pile.

All the previous year's offerings were still included in the 1961 catalogue – although it is interesting to note that the illustration used for the Traditional Teddy Bears had been changed to the plumper, cuddlier version first seen in the mid-1930s. Again, however, there were new designs as well – this time two novelties.

The 9 inch (23cm) Chime Bear was intended as a cot toy. Made in either pink or blue nylon plush, he had a cylindrical body and no legs, and had a musical chime inside his body. Aimed at slightly older children, on the other hand, was another muff, this time a Muff Sooty. Measuring 14 inches (35.5cm), his form was similar to that of the Muff Bear, but with a Sooty head instead of a Cheeky-style one. The muff, head and limbs were all in gold mohair, with black ears and with pads made from brown felt. A wand was clasped between Sooty's paws, which again were hinged onto the body, as were the legs. The muff itself was lined with silk.

1962

A year later, however, the only Sooty still being offered in the Merrythought catalogue was the "glove puppet" type of sachet. The Muff Bear had gone as well, and there were many other changes – not least a totally new kind of spiral-bound catalogue. The brand-new photos gave a much more accurate image of those toys that had been in the range for a number of years. Some of them had evolved constantly in response to changing tastes and the arrival of new fabrics, but the changes had not previously been shown in the catalogue illustrations.

Now there were two new photos of the Traditional ("M" series) Teddy Bears, for instance, which were still offered in the same five sizes. One illustration clearly showed a fairly large example, with shapely legs and relatively long, upward curving arms. But one was obviously smaller, and his shape was noticeably different. The limbs were short and stubby, and relatively straight, while his ears were disproportionately large in comparison with those of his big brother, almost meeting

The Chime Bear, first on offer in 1961, was available in either blue or pink, and contained a musical chime.

The 1961 Muff Sooty was similar in design to the Muff Bear, and was made from gold mohair. Originally he carried a wand in his paw.

This giant Yogi is the same size as the Showpiece version but is in the form of a nightdress case, which was never included in the Merrythought catalogue.

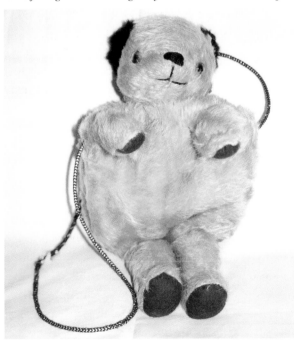

47

on the top of his head. He was, in other words, a typical sixties bear.

Also still on offer in 1962 were various Cheekys (see separate chapter), as well as the Koala Bear in Australian skin, the nylon Chime Bear and the mohair Miniature Bear. There was, however, a new look for the fully washable Jumpee Bear, which now had body and muzzle in contrasting nylon.

There was also a distinctive and wholly new top-of-the-range design, known as the Peter Bear. Made from a long-pile mohair, with jointed arms and head, he was 13 inches (33cm) in height and had an inset velveteen face as well as velveteen feet. Sideways glancing eyes gave added character.

The same year also saw the appearance of the first Merrythought Yogi Bears, available only in the UK. Most measured 11 inches (28cm) in height, but there was a

giant 27 inch (68.5cm) "Showpiece" version too, which today is far more rare. The unjointed bears were made in assorted shades of velveteen, with muzzles in a contrasting shade. The eyes were black and white felt, the legs short with large feet, and thin arms were hinged onto the shoulders. A felt boater and a white plastic collar with ribbon tie completed the look.

In 1963, another Yogi was added to the range – this time seated on a bright red tricycle. He was based on the smaller-sized version of the original Yogi, but the body was shortened and the legs lengthened to enable them to reach the pedals, to which they were attached. The legs were hinged onto the body, and had an additional hinge at the knee. As the tricycle was pulled along, turning the pedals, the legs turned with them, giving the impression that the rider was pedalling furiously.

Many of the other bears in the range remained essentially unchanged that year, but the Sooty sachet had gone and there was a new pattern for the fully jointed

The unjointed Yogi Bears were made in assorted shades of velveteen from 1962 onwards. This one still has his original swing tag.

This classic ted, dating from around 1962-3, is made from alpaca with suedette pads and has his glass eyes firmly locked into place with a patented fastening.

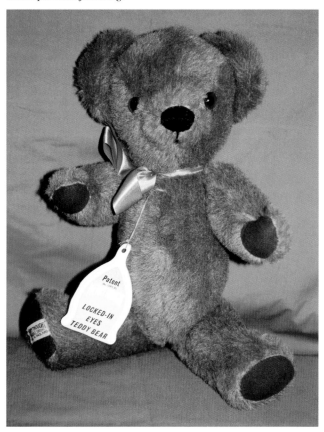

The changes to the bears in 1965 were more extensive – some of them minor variations on existing designs, others major innovations. The Koala Bear, for instance, was now being produced in an additional small size (5 inches/12.5cm). The mohair Miniature Bear was now available in assorted shades. There were new fabrics for some of the Cheekys, and the Traditional Teddy Bears were now available in two different qualities. The code NM was reserved for those made in a "Rich golden shaggy mohair", while a new GM code was given to a version in "Super London gold pure mohair". Both were offered in the same five sizes as the previous NM Bears, and could be fitted with "tip up growlers" or music boxes as required.

The Danish comic strip character Rasmus Klump (known in Germany as Petzi) was the inspiration behind the 1962 Peter Bear, which had an inset face made from velveteen.

Traditional Teddy Bears. Gone were the relatively pronounced and shaved noses of the earlier bears. The faces were now flatter, and the limbs had become quite short and straight, even on the larger sizes. Called simply the NM Bear, the new design was offered in a total of five sizes, ranging from 14 to 32 inches (35.5 to 81cm). All were made from mohair, and with a very soft kapok filling.

By the time the 1964 catalogue appeared, Peter Bear was notable by his absence. So, too, was Yogi on his tricycle. But there was a new addition to the Cheeky range (see *Cheeky little bear*) and also one brand-new design – a nightdress case Super Bear, available in cream or white synthetic plush. Measuring 21 inches (53.5cm) in length, he appears from the catalogue photograph to be an unjointed, soft-stuffed and cuddly teddy, with space inside his body to hold the child's nightwear, and a zip fastener in his back.

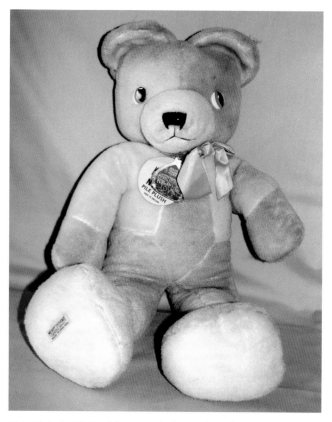

This 21 inch (53.5cm) bear, made from nylon plush, was created in the mid 1960s but was never included in the catalogue; only a few, if any, were ever sold.

There were changes to the Jumpee Bear, too – now called the Jumpee Sitting Bear, and measuring a slightly smaller 10 inches (25.5cm). Still made from nylon with white tummy, muzzle, ear linings and foot pads, the new design was again unjointed but had noticeably longer

The Jumpee Sitting Bears, introduced in 1965, were never offered in this type of plush in the catalogue. This example was bought by one of the Merrythought employees.

The original Mr and Mrs Twisty Bear were in art silk, with removable, brightly coloured clothes made from felt - missing from this rare example.

This version of Mr and Mrs Twisty Bear was first seen in 1966; only the heads were mohair, with contrasting white plush muzzles.

and upward curving arms, which no doubt made him extra huggable. The Trials Book refers to "an amalgam of best teddy features of past designs".

The Yogi Bears, on the other hand, had disappeared completely, but the Chime Bear appeared essentially unchanged, as did the Super Bear nightdress case. The catalogue also noted that another teddy nightdress case of similar size was available in London Gold mohair.

The most innovative of the new teddies were, however, Mr and Mrs Twisty Bear. Instead of being fitted with conventional disc jointing, they had a new internal "Flexible frame", enabling them to be "manipulated into any position". The arms, for instance, could be bent or straightened, twisted up and down or forwards and back. There were two sizes - 11 inches (28cm) and a giant 24 inch (61cm) "Showpiece" version.

Those shown in the 1965 catalogue were made from gold art silk with brightly coloured felt clothes - a skirt for her and trousers for him. By the following year, however, there had been some changes. The heads were in mohair - gold, with contrasting white plush muzzles - while the bodies and limbs were made of a soft turquoise cloth, with white paws and large black feet. Again they were dressed, with Mr Twisty Bear wearing red trousers and a white collar while Mrs Twisty Bear was given a red skirt topped with a white apron. Both were available in the same two sizes as the previous year's versions.

A Mr and Mrs Twisty Cheeky appeared that year too (see separate chapter on the Cheeky), but again many of the bears remained totally unchanged. The shaggy mohair version of the Traditional Teddy Bear was, however, no longer listed, and the Cheeky was also no longer available in this fabric (see Cheeky chapter).

New arrivals in 1966 included wheeled Pandas on all fours. There were two sizes. The largest, known as Push Toys, measured 27 inches (68.5cm) long and 25 inches (63.5cm) high, and came complete with chrome handles, foot rests and large tyres. The smaller size, known as Toddle Toys, measured 20 inches (51cm) in both length and height, and came without the extra features.

It is rare to find a Merrythought Winnie-the-Pooh still wearing his red shirt. The fully jointed, mohair bears were first seen in 1966.

There was another Panda, this time sitting, in the nightdress case section. Measuring 16 inches (40.5cm) in height, he was made from black and white "silk plush" and was said to have an "ample zip pocket".

The most interesting new arrivals of the year, however, were Merrythought versions of Winnie-the-Pooh along with his friends Kanga (and Roo), Eeyore and Piglet, to coincide with the release of a Walt Disney film. Pooh himself was a fully jointed 10 inch (25.5cm) bear, made from gold mohair and wearing a red felt shirt on

which the name Pooh had been printed. There was a giant 'Showpiece' version as well, measuring 24 inches (61cm), and a nightdress case Pooh is included on a list of additional lines not illustrated in the catalogue.

Chime versions of Winnie-the-Pooh and some of his friends were introduced in 1967. They had no legs, and a cylindrical body containing the musical chime.

Winnie-the-Pooh and his friends were strongly featured in the 1967 catalogue as well, with Tigger, Wol and Rabbit all being produced alongside the existing characters. There were Chime versions of Pooh, Kanga, Wol and Piglet too, each measuring 9 inches (23cm) high. The Chime Pooh was made from mohair, with a red shirt on which his name was printed.

A 21 inch (53.5cm) Pooh-shaped nightdress case had been a late addition to the previous year's range. In 1967 it was joined by a "Pooh in Bed" sachet. A red velveteen quilted bed was topped with a white satin pillow on which the name Pooh had been inscribed. Attached to the pillow were head and paws made from mohair, while mohair feet appeared to be poking out from under the bottom of the quilt. A zipped pocket held the child's nightwear.

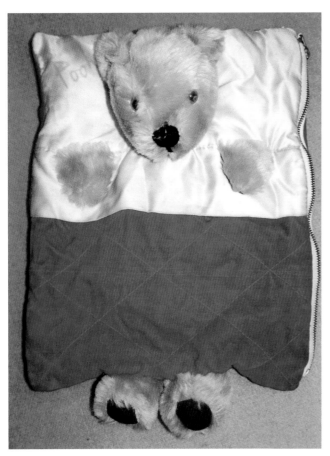

The "Pooh in Bed" sachet was one of many nightdress cases to be produced by Merrythought. The bed was made from satin and quilted velveteen, while the bear's head and feet were mohair.

This 21 inch (53.5cm) nightdress case was made from the same pattern as the Super Bear, which was produced in a variety of fabrics including both mohair and synthetics. This version never appeared in the catalogue.

With the arrival of the Pooh-shaped mohair nightdress case, the earlier London Gold teddy nightdress case disappeared, but the Super Bear in cream or white plush was still available. There was also a 16 inch (40.5cm) Koala Bear case – made, like the Koala toys, from "real skin" and fitted with a zip-fastened, lined pocket in the back.

Several other bear-related designs remained unchanged, but the Jumpee Bear had reverted to one that was similar to the pre-1965 version, while the Chime Bear and wheeled Pandas were no longer shown. The Chime Bear would, however, return the following year, in a slightly modified design.

The Chime Pooh and his friends, on the other hand, disappeared in 1968, as did the cream version of the Super Bear nightdress case. There were some changes to the Koalas as well; these were still made from real skins, but were now in different sizes (5, 7, 9 and 11 inches, or

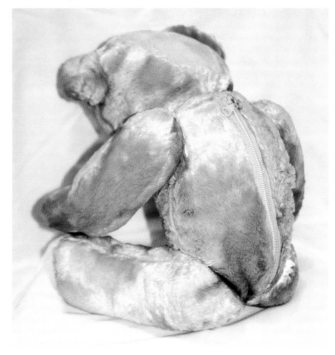

12.5, 18, 23 and 28cm). Other designs remained unchanged, although the Jumpee Bear had been renamed the Merry Bear – one of a whole range of Jumpee Toys. The Jumpee name was dropped completely in 1969.

The biggest change in 1969, however, was the disappearance of much of the Winnie-the-Pooh range. Winnie-the-Pooh himself was still available, in regular and "Showpiece" sizes, but of his friends only Eeyore and Kanga (with Roo) remained – Kanga-&-Roo still also in a "showpiece" size. The Pooh-shaped nightdress case had been dropped as well, although the Pooh in Bed sachet was still on offer.

Mr and Mrs Twisty Cheeky were also no longer shown, but Mr and Mrs Twisty Bear remained – although they were now described as "Made in first quality plushes in bright and appealing colours". Both the Traditional Teddy Bears and the Cheeky were likewise still available – and still in the same sizes and fabrics as in

1968. The Koala Bears, the Miniature Bear, the Chime Bear, the Merry Bear, and the white Super Bear nightdress case were all there too. However, it is possible that some of the fabrics may have changed from those used in previous years.

Totally new, on the other hand, was an upright Polar Bear in "long white realistic plush", measuring a hefty 22 inches (56cm) and with a cub held in her right paw. There was a new Panda on all fours as well – 14 inches (35.5cm) long and made from black and white silk plushes. In addition, a Panda on all fours was included among the new nightdress cases. Measuring 18 inches (45.5cm) in length, he had a zip fastener along the top of his back, which could be opened to reveal the lined pocket inside.

The 1960s had seen many changes in Merrythought's range of bear-related toys – but still more would follow in the decade to come.

The swing tag on this 1960s mohair bear advertises his locked-in eyes, which were made from glass. Merrythought patented the special fastening that kept the eyes firmly in place.

This mohair ted is typical of those made by Merrythought during the 1960s. Glass eyes would indicate that he was made early in the decade; plastic eyes (as here) suggest later.

Traditional Merrythought Bears

1960
[The illustration was identical to that which appeared in the 1950 catalogue]
Traditional Teddy Bears
"M" Bears made from pure mohair in sizes 14, 16, 18, 21 and 30 inches (35.5, 40.5, 45.5, 53.5 and 76cm)

1961
[The illustration was identical to that used for the 1930s "M" series bears]
Traditional Teddy Bears
"M" Bears made from pure mohair in sizes 14, 16, 18, 21 and 30 inches (35.5, 40.5, 45.5, 53.5 and 76cm)

1962
Traditional Teddy Bears
Made from pure mohair in sizes 14, 16, 18, 21 and 30 inches (35.5, 40.5, 45.5, 53.5 and 76cm)

1963, 1964
Traditional Teddy Bears
"NM" Bears made from mohair in sizes 14, 16, 18, 21 and 32 inches (35.5, 40.5, 45.5, 53.5 and 81cm)

1965
Traditional Teddy Bears
"NM" Bears made from rich golden shaggy mohair in sizes 14, 16, 18, 21 and 32 inches (35.5, 40.5, 45.5, 53.5 and 81cm)

"GM" Bears made from London gold mohair in sizes 14, 16, 18, 21 and 32 inches (35.5, 40.5, 45.5, 53.5 and 81cm)

1966, 1967
Traditional Teddy Bears
"GM" Bears made from London gold mohair in sizes 14, 16, 18, 21 and 32 inches (35.5, 40.5, 45.5, 53.5 and 81cm)

1968, 1969
Traditional Teddy Bears
"GM" Bears made from Old Gold mohair in sizes 14, 16, 18, 21 and 32 inches (35.5, 40.5, 45.5, 53.5 and 81cm)

Chapter 5

5. THE 1970s
1970

By 1970, the number of fully jointed mohair bears being made by British soft toy manufacturers was dwindling fast. Most makers were concentrating instead on unjointed teddies in the new synthetic fabrics. These were cheaper to produce than the traditional designs, and many firms saw them as the only possible way of competing with the huge numbers of inexpensive cuddly toys being imported from the Far East.

This "Super simulated mink Teddy Bear nightdress case" is as he appeared in the 1971 catalogue. He measured 22 inches (56cm).

Merrythought, however, adopted a different tack, and one which would ultimately prove far more successful. They opted for quality. Bears in "Best quality mohair" remained an important part of the range, although the same designs were often offered in good synthetic fabrics as well.

Many of the bears in the 1970 catalogue were identical or similar to those on sale in 1969, but there were some changes to the fabrics used for both the Traditional Bears and the Cheeky. The former was still being made in Old Gold mohair, for instance, in a total of five sizes ranging from 14 to 32 inches (35.5 to 81cm). But there was also now a version in synthetic "Light champagne mink plush", in the same five sizes. All could be fitted with tip-up growlers. The Cheeky was also still available in gold mohair, but the art silk version had given way to one in another synthetic plush. A new Muff Bear with a Cheeky head was also offered. (See *Cheeky little bear* for further details.)

Apparently unchanged, on the other hand, were Winnie-the-Pooh (including the Pooh in Bed sachet) along with his friends Eeyore and Kanga-&-Roo. The Miniature Bear in mohair, the Standing Panda and the Koala Bears were likewise old favourites, but gone were the Chime Bear and the Polar Bear and Cub. The 11 inch (28cm) version of the Merry Bear was missing as well, but had been replaced by 12, 24 and 36 inch sizes (30.5, 61 and 91.5cm). There were also changes to the description of Mr and Mrs Twisty Bear, now given as being made from "best quality Red Nylon plush". Both were still 11 inches (28cm) in height, with 24 inch (61cm) "Showpieces" also available.

A simulated mink fabric was used for both Cheeky Bears and more traditional teddies in the early 1970s.

The London Guardsman of the 1970s had head, hands and feet of brown mohair; his clothing formed his body and limbs.

The Panda nightdress case was still being made too, but the Super Bear in "long white plush" had been replaced by one in either "dark mink plush" or "light Champagne super quality plush".

In 1971, the Traditional Bear fabrics were given as "best quality mohair" and "simulated mink", but were actually identical to those of the previous year. New, on the other hand, was a giant 48 inch (122cm) size in both qualities. There were also some changes to the fabrics used for the Cheeky Bears (see *Cheeky little bear*), although the mohair version was again unaltered.

There were no apparent changes to Winnie-the-Pooh and his friends (including the Pooh in Bed sachet), or to the Muff Bear, the Merry Bear, Mr and Mrs Twisty Bear, the Miniature Bear or the Koala Bears (still said to be realistic models and made out of real skins). But the Panda nightdress case had disappeared, and the only Bear nightdress case offered was that in simulated mink. Yogi

Bear was back, however, in 11 and 27 inch sizes (28 and 68.5cm) and in assorted shades of velveteen.

Totally new were some smiling Sticky Bears, with heads and feet made of white nylon plush, and with soft-stuffed bodies made in brightly coloured nylon. Velcro pads were added to the hands to give extra "play value". The pads would stick to those on other Sticky Toys, or on the same bear.

In 1972 there were again relatively few changes. The Traditional Bears, the Cheekys, Winnie-the-Pooh and his friends (including Pooh in Bed), Yogi Bear, the Miniature Bear, the Muff Bear and the Bear nightdress case all appear to have been the same as those of the previous year. Of the Merry Bears, however, only the 12 inch (30.5cm) size remained, and it was now specified that the colours on offer were pastel pink and blue. Mr and Mrs Twisty Bear also disappeared that year, as did the short-lived Sticky Bears, and the photograph of the Koala

Apart from his clothing, the 1972 London Policeman was identical to the London Guardsman introduced at the same time, although the different headgear meant that they were different in height.

Bears suggests that they had undergone some modifications, although they were still being made from real skins.

A more significant development in 1972 was the introduction of two new dressed bears, based on the popular Bingies of the 1930s. The London Guardsman had head, hands and feet of "bear brown" mohair, but his body and limbs took the form of a bright red tunic and black trousers. On his head was an "Imitation thick pile Bearskin headpiece". Similarly, mohair was used only for the head, paws and feet of the London Policeman. Body and limbs were in the form of a policeman's uniform, and there was a policeman's helmet on his head. Both bears were unjointed, and made in two sizes – 21 or 30 inches (53.5 or 76cm) for the Guardsman, and 20 or 28 inches (51 or 71 cm) for the Policeman. The differences in sizes came simply from the difference in size of their headgear.

In 1973, the London Guardsman and London Policeman were joined by a Beefeater in a red costume trimmed with yellow and black braid. The head and paws were in gold mohair.

This Highlander, with tartan kilt and tam-o'shanter, was first seen in 1973.

Both seem to have been popular, and a year later they had been joined by a Beefeater with smart red coat and trousers, trimmed with yellow and black braid. He wore a black Beefeater's hat trimmed in red, white and blue, and instead of mohair feet he had black shoes. There was a new Highlander too, with tartan kilt and tam-o'shanter, a black "shirt", and snowy white sporran. In his case, however, mohair was used for the legs and feet as well as the head and hands. Both new bears were, like the two original designs, available in two sizes, this time 18 and 25 inches (45.5 and 63.5cm).

Most of the other 1973 bears were identical to those of the previous year, although there was a new 16 inch (40.5cm) Standing Panda in nylon plush. There was also a new Panda nightdress case, measuring 22 inches (56cm) long, and made from black and white nylon plushes with a zip along his back. Instead of standing sturdily on all fours, he was in a crouching position with his head resting on his front paws.

however, no other omissions among the bears, although a couple of new designs had been added. A pair of Flexi Bears – a boy and a girl made from yellow plush with bright red clothes – were included in the new range of Flexi toys. These had their arms, legs and heads reinforced with a "safety wire frame", so that the limbs could be "flexed" into a variety of positions.

There was also a new Floppy Panda, 24 inches (60cm) in length and made from black and white simulated mink "to give natural markings". A year later, though, he was no longer shown in the catalogue, which now included a 27 inch (68.5cm) Floppy Polar Bear in "lush white plush with embroidered nose and paw markings", which was also available as a nightdress case.

The brown "Dreylon" versions of the Traditional and Cheeky Bears were also missing from the 1976 catalogue. So too were the London Guardsman and the Beefeater, as well as the boy and girl Flexi Bears. The little mohair Miniature Bear "for the smallest child" had gone too, but in his place was a 7 inch (18cm) unjointed mohair Baby Bear – said to be "a tiny teddy for the very young".

For a short while during the early 1970s, Merrythought produced some fully jointed mohair bears without the usual seam down the front of the body.

Albert was a character in a series of children's books by Alison Jezard. Merrythought produced just a few examples of an Albert soft toy in the early 1970s.

Both Pandas remained in the range for just a year, during which time there was also a significant change to the Koala Bears. In the 1974 catalogue the "real skins" were replaced by an "alpaca mixture pile plush of natural colouring", with the animals being made in 6, 8 and 10 inch sizes (15, 20.5 and 25.5 cm).

Yogi Bear, Winnie-the-Pooh (including the Pooh in Bed sachet) and Eeyore were also absent from the 1974 catalogue, although Kanga-&-Roo were still included. Gone too was the Merry Bear, but the Miniature Bear, the Muff Bear and the Bear nightdress case all remained. The four dressed bears were still there as well, as were the Traditional and Cheeky Bears in both mohair and simulated mink. But the latter two designs were also now available in "brown Dreylon" – each in a total of six sizes.

The range of Traditional and Cheeky Bears for 1975 was the same, but of the dressed bears only the London Guardsman and Beefeater remained. There were,

The simulated mink bears date from the early 1970s, but remained on sale for over a decade; the square swing tag on this one suggests that he is a late 1970s example.

The Flexi Bear Boy dates from 1975, and was made from lemon and white nylon with felt dungarees.

A 7 inch (18cm) unjointed Baby Bear, made from mohair, took the place of the earlier Miniature Bear in 1976. Like its predecessor, it was unjointed.

This fully jointed mohair bear dates from the late 1970s, when they continued to be made in a wide range of sizes.

Unchanged, on the other hand, were the Muff Bear and the Bear nightdress case in simulated mink. The three sizes of Koala Bear were also still on offer, although their fabric was now described as "alpaca/mohair" rather than "alpaca mixture". In addition, Winnie-the-Pooh was back, still wearing a bright red felt jacket with his name on the front. With him were his friends Eeyore, Kanga-&-Roo, Tigger and Piglet, with all but Piglet also available in large "Showpiece" sizes.

This time they remained on offer for just a year, and would not return. The Muff Bear and the Koala Bears disappeared with them, but the Traditional and Cheeky Bears remained unchanged in 1977, and a new Bed-time Bear with a Cheeky head was also introduced (see *Cheeky little bear*). The Baby Bear, Bear nightdress case,

and the Floppy Polar Bears (including nightdress case) were retained as well.

The only changes in 1978 were the disappearance of the Bed-time Bear and the arrival of a 16 inch (40.5cm) Koala with Baby in "fine plushes", with the baby nestling in the mother's arms. In 1979, too, changes to the bears were minimal. There was a new 12 inch (30.5cm) Standing Bear on all fours, in brown and cream plushes. A Koala Bear nightdress case had also been added to the range – made from brown plush with a honey-coloured chest. But all the bears from the 1978 catalogue were still included. Even at the end of the decade, Merrythought were continuing to offer fully jointed mohair bears alongside unjointed toys in the newer synthetics.

The Traditional Teddy Bears

1970
Old Gold mohair in sizes 14, 16, 18, 21 and 32 inches (35.5, 40.5, 45.5, 53.5 and 81cm)
Light Champagne Mink plush in sizes 14, 16, 18, 21 and 32 inches (35.5, 40.5, 45.5, 53.5 and 81cm)

1971, 1972, 1973
Best quality mohair in sizes 14, 16, 18, 21, 32 and 48 inches (35.5, 40.5, 45.5, 53.5, 81 and 122cm)
Simulated Mink in sizes 14, 16, 18, 21, 32 and 48 inches (35.5, 40.5, 45.5, 53.5, 81 and 122cm)

1974
London Gold mohair in sizes 14, 16, 18, 21, 32 and 48 inches (35.5, 40.5, 45.5, 53.5, 81 and 122cm)
Simulated Mink in sizes 14, 16, 18, 21, 32 and 48 inches (35.5, 40.5, 45.5, 53.5, 81 and 122cm)
Brown "Dreylon" in sizes 14, 16, 18, 21, 32 and 48 inches (35.5, 40.5, 45.5, 53.5, 81 and 122cm)

1975
London Gold mohair in sizes 10, 14, 16, 18, 21, 32 and 48 inches (25.5, 35.5, 40.5, 45.5, 53.5, 81 and 122cm)
Simulated Mink in sizes 14, 16, 18, 21, 32 and 48 inches (35.5, 40.5, 45.5, 53.5, 81 and 122cm)
Brown "Dreylon" in sizes 14, 16, 18, 21, 32 and 48 inches (35.5, 40.5, 45.5, 53.5, 81 and 122cm)

1976
London Gold mohair in sizes 10, 14, 16, 18, 21, 32 and 48 inches (25.5, 35.5, 40.5, 45.5, 53.5, 81 and 122cm)
Simulated Mink in sizes 14, 16, 18, 21, 32 and 48 inches (35.5, 40.5, 45.5, 53.5, 81 and 122cm)

1977, 1978, 1979
London Gold mohair blend in sizes 10, 14, 16, 18, 21, 32 and 48 inches (25.5, 35.5, 40.5, 45.5, 53.5, 81 and 122cm)
Simulated Mink in sizes 14, 16, 18, 21, 32 and 48 inches (35.5, 40.5, 45.5, 53.5, 81 and 122cm)

Chapter 6

6. THE 1980s

1980–2

Merrythought celebrated its golden jubilee in 1980. But although the front of the catalogue marked the occasion by giving the dates 1930-1980 under the company name, there appears to have been no further fanfare. There were no Jubilee Bears or other special commemorative items shown. Instead, Merrythought simply carried on offering its usual mix of high-quality toys, although many other companies at the time were turning out increasing numbers of cheap and cheerful lines to try and compete with inexpensive imported toys.

The "M" Series Traditional Bears and the Cheekys were identical to those of 1979, available in either a London Gold mohair blend or in simulated mink. The Bear nightdress case in simulated mink was still there as well, and so was the 7 inch (18cm) Baby Bear. There were no other teddy-type bears on offer, however, although there were some more "realistic" bears, as well as pandas and koalas.

The GM series of fully jointed bears in London Gold mohair was a fixture in the range throughout the 1980s.

The Mother and Baby Koalas were still available, for instance, and also the Floppy Polar Bears, including the nightdress case. So were the Standing Bear and the Koala Bear nightdress case. But there was a new 15 inch (38cm) Panda nightdress case as well – made in "realistic black and white", and again with a zipped pocket in the body to hold a child's nightwear.

Also new was an unjointed sitting Panda, in black and white synthetic plushes and stuffed with kapok. It was available in three sizes (12, 15 and 30 inches, or 30.5, 38 and 76cm).

In 1981, the 10 inch (25.5cm) Traditional Bear disappeared and there was a new 13 inch (33cm) version of the simulated mink Cheeky. The Baby Bear was unchanged, as were the unjointed Pandas, the Floppy Polar Bears (including nightdress case) and the Standing Bear, but the Mother and Baby Koalas had disappeared and so had the Koala nightdress case. Gone, too, was the Bear nightdress case made from simulated mink, although that in the form of a Panda still remained. Totally new, on the other hand, was a Standing Bear on all fours, measuring 12 inches (30cm) in length and made from brown and cream plushes, with a kapok filling.

The following year, one of the most significant changes was to the catalogue itself. All the descriptions of the toys were omitted. Instead, the pages were filled simply with photographs of each part of the range, with the toys identified only by a code of two or three letters. The names of the toys, and the sizes available, were given on the accompanying price list, and there was no information as to materials used or any other characteristics. The fact that the 1982 price list is today missing from the company archives makes it even harder to determine exactly what was available that year – although the full-colour photos are more informative than the black and white that was still used for many illustrations up to the previous year.

It is clear, however, that the Traditional Bears in London Gold mohair were still there in 1982, although the simulated mink version appears to have been replaced by a new Champagne Luxury Bear in synthetic fabric. Two of the pictured bears are also wearing bibs, one of which carries the words "I Growl" and the other "I

The London Gold Bear and Champagne Luxury Bear, as featured on the front of the 1983 catalogue.

This polar bear, in two sizes, remained on sale for much of the 1980s. He was unjointed, and made from a synthetic plush.

play a tune". It appears from details in later catalogues that the 18 inch (45.5cm) versions of both the London Gold and the Champagne Luxury Bears could be ordered with growlers or music boxes if desired.

There were new fabrics for the Cheeky as well (see *Cheeky little bear* chapter), and it appears that the Pandas were now available in four sizes. Again, later price lists give a clue, as they include a 9.5 inch (24cm) version in addition to the original three sizes.

The Panda nightdress case is again shown as well, and there are two upright Polar Bears – one around twice the height of the other. The Trials Book suggests, however, that these are not a mother and baby but a standard sized toy and a "Showpiece" version.

A year later, in the 1983 catalogue, they had been replaced by examples in 12 and 18 inch (30.5 and 45.5cm) sizes. The Pandas, including the nightdress case, remained unchanged, but the bears did see a few alterations.

The London Gold Traditional Bears were still there, in sizes 12, 14, 16, 18, 21, 32 and 40 inches (30.5, 35.5, 40.5, 45.5. 53.5, 81 and 101.5cm). So were the Champagne Luxury Bears, in the six larger sizes, and the 18 inch (45.5cm) versions of each could again be fitted with growlers or music boxes. But there was a new "S series"

In 1983 there was a new series of fully jointed bears, made from a synthetic plush, known as the Aristocrat Bears. They had shaved muzzles and the nose stitching was of a type used in the 1930s.

The fully jointed Champagne Luxury Bear was made from 1983 to 1988 in various sizes, and took his name from the colour of his synthetic plush.

of Aristocrat Bears, whose most distinctive features were their shaved muzzles and changed nose stitching – both reminiscent of those seen in the 1930s. They were made in a pale beige plush (referred to in later catalogues as cinnamon), in the same six sizes as the Champagne Luxury Bears, and with growlers or music boxes again a possible addition for the 18 inch (45.5cm) version.

There were some minor changes to the Cheekys as well (see separate chapter), and this range would also undergo some small modifications the following year. But in 1984 it was again the Traditional Bears that saw the most significant changes. The London Gold and Champagne Luxury variations were unaltered, apart from a new 12 inch (30.5cm) Champagne size, but they were joined by a second gold version – this time not in mohair but in synthetic plush. Known simply as the Gold Traditional Bear, it was available in the same range of sizes as the other two Traditional Bears, and again with the possibility of growlers or music boxes in the 18 inch (45.5cm) version.

There were changes to the Aristocrat Bears too. Now only three sizes were available, namely 14, 16 and 18 inches (35.5, 40.5 and 45.5cm), and none had growlers or music boxes.

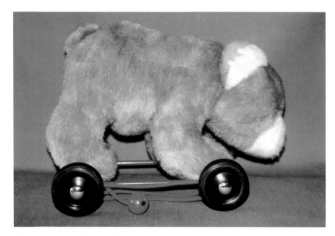

The pull-along Roller Bear was on sale for just one year, 1984. Made from synthetic plush, he was unjointed and measured 9 inches (23cm) in length.

On the other hand, the Polar Bears and sitting Pandas (including the nightdress case) appeared unchanged from those of the previous year. But new Koala Bears had been added to the range, with three sizes of cuddly toy (6, 8 and 13 inches/15, 20.5 and 33cm) as well as a new nightdress case. There was also a brand-new little 9 inch (23cm) Pull-along Roller Bear on wheels.

The Roller Bear had disappeared by the following year (1985), but the Polar Bears, Pandas and Koalas were all still there, including the Koala Bear nightdress case (although the design of the Koalas had been modified). They had also been joined by new Softie Pandas and Softie Polar Bears that were unjointed and ultra cuddly, and available in 15 and 24 inch sizes (38 and 61cm). There were new Softie Bears as well – all three animals being made from the same body pattern but with different heads.

The Aristocrats remained in the range too, and were unchanged from the previous year. Also unchanged were the London Gold jointed bears (in both mohair and synthetic plush) and the Champagne Luxury Bear. But

The 1986 Nutmeg Bear was a new, fully jointed bear in synthetic plush, with a plastic nose instead of the more usual stitched one.

In 1985, Merrythought brought out a new, fully jointed, mohair bear in "Ironbridge grey", which was available in seven sizes. This one measured 12 inches (30.5cm).

there had been a few changes to the sizes of Cheeky on offer (see *Cheeky little bear*), and there was also a new fully jointed bear. Again available in a total of seven sizes, with the possibility of growlers or music boxes in the middle size, the new arrival was a second mohair bear, this time in "Ironbridge grey". It would be available for just one year.

In 1986, the changes to the range were more far-reaching. Most striking was the disappearance of the

Cheeky after nearly 30 years. The Aristocrats had gone too, as had the Ironbridge grey mohair bears, the Softie Bears, Softie Pandas and Softie Polar Bears, and all the previous year's Koala Bears (including the nightdress case). The other three jointed bears – in London Gold mohair, London Gold synthetic plush and Champagne synthetic plush – were all still available, however, as were the upright Polar Bear (in two sizes), the sitting Panda (three sizes) and the sitting Panda nightdress case. Alongside them were a whole host of new designs.

There was a new jointed bear, for instance, with a more pronounced snout than that of the other jointed bears. His ears were also more cupped, he had a plastic nose, and there were other more subtle changes to his form. Made in 18, 22 and 26 inch sizes (45.5, 56 and 66cm), he was known as the Nutmeg Bear, taking his name from the colour of his synthetic plush.

Also new was an unjointed sitting teddy called Bobby Bear. Made from gold synthetic plush, he was offered in

7. A NEW DIRECTION

Up until the early 1980s, all of Merrythought's bears and other animals had been made purely with children in mind. Some had certainly found their way into adult collections, but they had never been created specifically for that purpose. Then, in 1983, the company received a special request from their American distributors Tide-Rider. Could they produce a numbered, signed, limited-edition bear for the growing American collectors market? The move would eventually lead to a whole new era of Merrythought toy making.

Tide-Rider, a small import business, had been founded in 1950 by Harry Klein. Initially they had imported sports equipment from the UK, but in the late fifties and early sixties they had expanded their area of interest to include a range of puppets from Britain and toy sailboats from Germany. Then, in the late seventies, the business was acquired by the founder's daughter Linda Smith and her husband Jim. They added teddy bears and, later, collectable dolls to the Tide-Rider range.

That was when the association with Merrythought began. It so happened that Merrythought were looking to expand their distribution in the United States, and the British Trade Council duly contacted Tide-Rider to see if they would be interested in representing the British company. Merrythought's Oliver Holmes telephoned Linda Smith soon afterwards, and arranged to meet her at a toy fair in California. He took with him a Cheeky and other classic bears as samples of his company's work. Linda liked what she saw and Tide-Rider became the sole distributor for all Merrythought soft toys in the United States.

From 1978 until 1982, they sold regular Merrythought lines and also the popular Cheeky. But by the early eighties, Linda had started to notice a new trend in the US – an interest in bears as collectables. In Britain, adult enthusiasts were still few and far between. In America, on the other hand, the number was growing fast and, after some years of selling quality bears, Linda knew just what these new buyers wanted. She asked whether Merrythought would create a limited edition specially for them, with each bear individually numbered.

At that time, what most collectors were after was old-style, fully jointed bears made from traditional mohair –

The 1983 Edwardian Bears. All were fully jointed and made from British mohair. Left and centre: Two unlimited versions in short-pile fur, measuring 14 and 18 inches (35.5 and 45.5cm). Right: This 18 inch (45.5cm) version, made from a longer-pile fabric, was limited to 1,000; each was numbered and boxed, and the labels were signed by Merrythought chairman Trayton Holmes. Both the larger versions were fitted with growlers.

just like the ones their parents and grandparents had played with as children. Merrythought's designer Jacqueline Revitt knew exactly what would appeal to them. She created the Edwardian – a real aristocrat of a bear, based on those sold in Britain during the early twentieth century, in the reign of Edward VII.

There were three versions in all, each one fully jointed and made from pure English mohair with felt pads. The muzzles were shaved, with embroidered noses – their outside stitches extended slightly upwards – and the webbed claw stitching on the paws was reminiscent of that used on the early Farnells. Two of the Edwardian Bears, measuring 14 inches and 18 inches (35.5 and 45.5cm), were made in a short-pile bright gold fur, and neither of these were limited. But the third, an 18 inch (45.5cm) version in an antique style longer-pile mohair, was restricted to just 1,000. Boxed and individually numbered, they also had their sewn-in labels signed by Merrythought's then chairman Mr B.T. Holmes.

This 1984 set of four bears represented the four seasons. Left to right: Teacher's Pet (fall), Blossom (spring), Jingle (winter) and Sunshine (summer). Individually numbered and boxed, they were signed by Mr B.T. Holmes and were limited to 1,000 sets.

All three were made specially for the American market and all proved a huge success. The limited edition sold out entirely, paving the way for many more throughout the 1980s. Every single one of these was another sell-out. They included other new versions of the popular Edwardian, but alongside them were a host of totally different designs.

In 1984, for instance, a 14 inch (35.5cm) cinnamon-coloured Edwardian Bear was produced in a limited edition of 2,500. But the range that year also included a

16 inch (40.5cm) ted whose relatively long and pointed nose earned him the name Snout Bear. Fully jointed and made from an old gold shade of mohair, he was again limited to 2,500, with each of the numbered tags signed by Merrythought's chairman.

Different again was a set of four 14 inch (35.5cm) bears made from short-pile mohair in various shades. Each was dressed to represent one of the four seasons and came complete with an appropriate accessory. The spring Blossom, for instance, was white, and wore a fetching pink dress and bonnet. Summer's Sunshine had beige fur, and was dressed for the beach in a pale lemon romper suit and straw hat. Teacher's Pet, representing autumn or fall, was ready for the new school term in jacket, shirt and another straw hat, while the winter Jingle was suitably festive in red waistcoat and fur-trimmed red headgear. Sold only as a boxed set, the Seasonal Bear Collection was limited to 1,000, and the individually numbered bears had again been signed by Mr B.T. Holmes.

A year later there were even more new arrivals, as the rapid growth of the American collectors market brought a continued increase in demand. This time, there was a cuddly gold Pair of Bears, measuring 11 and 14 inches (28 and 35.5 cm) and with all the features of the Edwardian Bears. A new 18 inch (45.5cm) Edwardian Bear in a long-pile cream mohair appeared as well, and later in the year there was a splendid Edwardian Surprise Brown Bear in a beautiful frosted fur. All were limited to 1,000.

The same year's range also included the Bearlington Family of three dressed bears. Sold as a set in a smart red display box, they too were restricted to just 1,000. The 16 inch (40.5cm) father bear was an Admiral, complete with gold braided jacket and hat, and with a monocle in his eye. Mother Victoria, 15 inches (38cm), wore a lace-trimmed dress and cap, while the 11 inch (28cm) baby had a smart sailor's outfit.

Another limited edition was introduced in time for Christmas. The 16 inch (40.5cm) Noel, again limited to 1,000, wore a festive red tunic – trimmed with white fur, and set off by a furry white hat.

New versions of the popular Edwardian Bears continued to appear in the years that followed, but in 1986 they were joined by a brand-new design: the Elizabethan Bear. This, too, would appear in many different forms in the years that followed, and again they would include many limited editions. Once more, characteristics included shaved noses and a distinctive form of claw stitching, but this time the claws appeared on the feet as well as the paws.

Among the first to appear was a 14 inch (35.5cm) version in a new tipped beige mohair, limited to just 1,000. There was also a 10 inch (25.5cm) Sailor Boy in blue and white sailor suit and cap, limited to 2,500, while Liberty's sash and crown made it plain that she was

Three of the Elizabethan bears. Left: The 15 inch (38cm) beige open-mouthed version was limited to just 500. Centre: The 14 inch (35.5cm) tipped beige bear was fitted with a growler and in a limited edition of 1,000. Right: The small white 11 inch (28cm) variant with dark brown ultrasuede pads was restricted to 500.

commemorating one hundred years of the Statue of Liberty. She, too, measured 10 inches (25.5cm) and was limited to 2,500. Later years would see further Elizabethans, including one with an open mouth.

The popularity of the 1985 Bearlington Family, on the other hand, led to a new set of "country cousins" – the Newbeary Family – in 1986. All were in spice brown mohair. Father Henry, measuring 16 inches (40.5cm), wore a striped shirt and corduroy trousers. The 14 inch (35.5cm) mother bear went by the name of Alma and was dressed in a white apron and red, lace-trimmed bonnet. The group was completed by baby Sadie, measuring just 11 inches (28cm), with bows in her ears and a pretty white and pink dress. Again they were sold only as a boxed set, with the edition limited to 1,000.

Best-remembered of all the 1986 newcomers, however, is the 10 inch (25.5cm) Ancestor of Cheeky with his mohair topknot and blue felt trunks. Fully jointed and made largely from a gold mohair and wool blend, his ear linings and the front of his body were white. He had the typical Cheeky-like grin on a velveteen muzzle, but the inspiration behind him was clearly the Cheeky's predecessor, Punkinhead, which had been made specially for Eaton's department store in Toronto, Canada, in the forties and fifties (see *Cheeky little bear*).

This 10 inch (25.5cm) Ancestor of Cheeky first appeared in 1986, and was produced in a limited edition of 1,000.

Illustrated on the title page of the new encyclopedia, for instance, was a classic Magnet Bear – or "the bear that attracts" – which had been made in numerous sizes and furs from the 1930s onwards. Now, original patterns were used to create a new 17 inch (43cm) mohair version in a soft honey-coloured shade, and in a limited edition of 1,000.

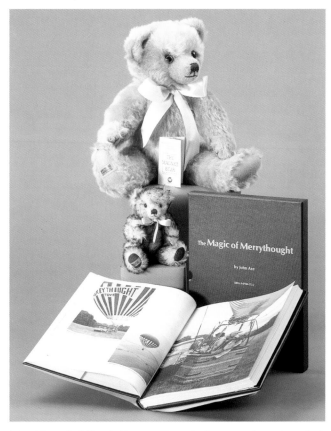

The 17 inch (43cm) Magnet Bear in honey-coloured mohair appeared in 1987 and was followed in 1988 by the 6 inch (15cm) tipped beige version. Each was limited to 1,000. The deluxe boxed edition of the book which inspired them – John Axe's The Magic of Merrythought *– was also limited, to 750.*

Another, more traditional, Merrythought found much greater fame in 1986, however, when he was given by Britain's Prince Edward to his brother Prince Andrew and Andrew's new wife Sarah Ferguson on their wedding day in July. As the couple set off for Heathrow at the start of their honeymoon, the 48 inch (122cm) giant ted was strapped into the carriage with them. He captured the imagination of bear lovers all over the world, but it was only those in America who were able to buy the 16 inch (40.5cm) copy that Merrythought made the following year. Made as a standing bear with flat feet, only his head and arms were jointed, and round his neck were two bows – one in pink and one in blue.

It was also in 1986 that John Axe's book on *The Magic of Merrythought* made its first appearance and this event, too, would have an impact on the new lines created by Merrythought for Tide-Rider in 1987. The book had featured hundreds of early Merrythought designs and now some of these, too, were re-created.

Another Magnet, this time in gold, was also one of three 6 inch (15cm) "Magic of Merrythought" Miniatures to appear in 1987, again inspired by the book. The others were a mohair Pimpo elephant (a smaller version of a 1933 design), and a standing terrier called Towzer (the full-size version of which had also appeared in 1933).

That year's Tide-Rider catalogue also included a new full-size replica of another old Merrythought bear. The original Prince Charlie had been featured in the 1987 edition of the annual Bialosky calendar. The limited-edition version, measuring 18 inches (45.5cm), was made

The 18 inch (45.5cm) Prince Charlie (right), in an old gold distressed mohair, was a replica of an old Merrythought bear owned by Ruth V. Kellar. He first appeared in 1987, and was limited to 1,000. Pictured with him is the 14 inch (35.5cm) cloaked Shakesbeare from 1988 – made in an edition of just 500. The reproduction of the 1932 catalogue also appeared that year.

in the new distressed mohair, in a beautiful shade of old gold. Restricted to 1,000, he was destined to become another collectors' classic.

Nearly all the new collectors bears were designed by Merrythought's Jacqueline Revitt, but the 1987 catalogue also included a pair of bears by one of the new and growing army of American teddy bear artists. The Chester Freeman™ Bears were named after their creator, a former chaplain. Fully jointed, and measuring 9 and 15 inches (23 and 38cm), they were made from a warm brown plush, with the larger of the two wearing a pair of gold-rimmed spectacles perched on the end of his distinctly aristocratic nose.

There was a new, unlimited, Mint Chocolate Chip in the 1987 catalogue as well, with paw stitching similar to that of the Elizabethan Bears. But it was the Edwardian style which came to the fore again in 1988. Three bolts of old mohair had been discovered hidden away in

Merrythought's attic. Each was slightly different in colour, and their age made them absolutely ideal for these well-loved traditional teds. As the fabric was strictly limited, so too were the editions – to just 500 each of the light blue, light grey and dark grey versions. Some black fabric, found at the same time, was also used to make a larger 25 inch (63.5cm) Edwardian – this time a mere 100 in all. The final touch was the signature of B. Trayton Holmes, the company's chairman, on the felt of one foot pad of each of the Edwardian Antique Fabric Bears.

The Edwardian Antique Fabric Bears from 1988 were all made from old mohair found in the Merrythought storerooms. The light blue, light grey and dark grey versions each measured 14 inches (35.5cm) and were limited to 500. The larger, 25 inch (63.5cm), black bear was in an edition of just 100.

The 1988 Wiltshire Bears were inspired by an old ted given to Tide-Rider's Linda Smith. Both measured 15 inches (38cm) and were limited to just 500.

There were two new additions to the "Magic of Merrythought" Miniatures in 1988 as well, this time a 1930s Dutch Bear and a classic golly. And it was another old bear which provided the inspiration for a new classic seen for the first time that year – the Wiltshire Bear. The original had been a gift to Tide-Rider's Linda Smith from a friend who lived in an old cottage in Wiltshire, England. The new versions were two 15 inch (38cm) limited editions in mohair. One was in a traditional short-pile gold fabric, the other in distressed old gold fur. Both were fully jointed and fitted with growlers, and the two editions were restricted to just 500 each.

In 1988 a cloaked Shakesbeare was another new arrival. There were also six new Clan Bears – traditional style, fully jointed teds made from vibrant coloured plush, and with scarves and tam-o'shanters in coordinating tartans. Each measured 14 inches (35.5cm). MacPherson and Fraser had heather-coloured fur, MacKenzie and Gordon a deep blue, while MacAlister and Dress Stuart were in a rich shade of green.

There were plans to extend the range further in the future, but the winds of change were already in the air. America was no longer the only country in which bears were collected. There was now a growing army of

The Edwardian British Virgin Wool Bears appeared in 1989. There were 14 inch (35.5cm) versions in gold, nutmeg and black, while the black was also used for a 25 inch (63.5cm) giant.

enthusiasts in other countries as well. Many of them saw the Tide-Rider advertisements in American magazines and were frustrated to find that the Merrythoughts featured in them were only available through American retailers. Many British collectors, in particular, found it hard to comprehend that these British-made creations were not on sale in their own country. Within two years, all that would have changed.

Meanwhile, however, there were still more new designs exclusive to Tide-Rider. Those in 1989, for instance, included yet more new Edwardians – this time a group of British Virgin Wool Bears, each wearing a pre-war metal wishbone (the Merrythought logo) in addition to their smart bows. There were 14 inch (35.5cm) gold, black and nutmeg versions, while the same black fur was also used for a 25 inch (63.5cm) big brother.

These two new Prince Charlie Bears appeared in 1989. That on the left was made from an "antique" chocolate mohair, discovered in the Merrythought storeroom. He was limited to just 100. The dark brown version with the shoulder bag was limited to 1,000. Both measured 18 inches (45.5cm).

There were two new versions of Prince Charlie as well – each, like the original, measuring 18 inches (45.5cm). One, in a rich shade of brown mohair, carried a small shoulder bag in the shape of a teddy's head, and was limited to 1,000. The other was made from another bolt of old fabric discovered in the Merrythought storeroom. With the fabric in short supply, the edition was restricted to just 100.

British Bertie, a 16 inch (40.5cm) character bear, was introduced in 1989 in a limited edition of 500.

The 18 inch (45.5cm) Jeremy, designed by John Axe, was actually available worldwide in a limited edition of 2,500. He won a prestigious Golden Teddy Award from the American magazine Teddy Bear Review.

British Bertie appeared in 1989 too – complete with bowler hat, briefcase and umbrella, and limited to just 500. But there was also the winsome Jeremy, designed by *The Magic of Merrythought* author John Axe and intended to have international appeal. Although few collectors outside the US knew of his existence at the time, Jeremy was not in fact an American exclusive. He was to be produced in a limited edition of 2,500 worldwide.

He appears to have received little attention outside the US, however, even though he went on to win a prestigious Golden Teddy Award from American specialist magazine *Teddy Bear Review*. This led to a new version – Jeremy Jr – wearing a Golden Teddy Award Rosette. It was this 14 inch (35.5cm) "baby", rather than the original 18 inch (45.5cm) size, which would become well-known on an international level after being included in the first

Merrythought International Collectors Catalogue in 1991.

Three other bears in that first international catalogue had likewise appeared in the 1989 Tide-Rider range. Two were Ironbridge Bears, another design destined to become a Merrythought classic. Launched in 1989, there were several versions made in open editions. But alongside them were two that were limited – one in apricot and the other in apricot tipped mohair. It was these two that were later also on offer in the first worldwide catalogue for collectors.

That international catalogue also included a 12 inch (30.5cm) Toffee Nose Bear. He, too, was already on sale in the US in 1989, although he was known as Toffe Bear then.

All the new Merrythought limited editions offered by Tide-Rider in 1990 were also listed in the 1991 international catalogue – among them the Ascot Bears, John Axe's Jeremy Jr and Isabel, and two perfumed Sachet Bears. It was, it seemed, the end of an era. It would be several years before Tide-Rider once again asked Merrythought to create some new designs especially for them.

The apricot and apricot tipped Ironbridge Bears, each limited to 1,000, appeared in the 1989 Tide-Rider catalogue – two years before they were included in the first Merrythought International Collectors Catalogue.

Chapter 8

8. CHEEKY LITTLE BEAR

He didn't have a name at first. In the Merrythought Trials Book, an entry on 5 October 1955 referred simply to a New Teddy. "Completely new range of bears," wrote designer Jean Barber. "Tubby Teddy ... very soft stuffed with amber eyes ... growls used according to style and price."

Punkinhead was made in three sizes for the Canadian department store Eaton's. This one, at 23 inches (58.5cm), was the largest.

Like many new designs, it would be modified before it made its first appearance, at a trade fair the following year. It was there that a royal visitor to the stand reputedly picked up one of the new toys to take a closer look. "What a cheeky little bear," she said as she noted his broad grin – and unwittingly gave him his name. Jean Barber added it to the description in the Trials Book, and the Cheeky was duly included in the next Merrythought catalogue for 1957. He would become one of the most enduring and best-loved of all the Merrythought designs.

Although he was recorded in the Trials Book as a Jean Barber original, however, the Cheeky had clearly been inspired by an earlier Merrythought favourite, made for a Canadian department store. In 1947, Eaton's in Toronto were looking for a new character to lead their annual Christmas parade. He would also appear in their Christmas catalogue, and they hoped he would help the store to compete with the hugely successful Rudolph the Red-Nosed Reindeer being used by one of their rivals. Their advertising department came up with several ideas, but it was finally decided that a comical bear would fit the bill perfectly.

Copywriter Beth Pringle wrote the story of *The Sad Little Bear*, a copy of which was given to every child who visited the store's Santa that Christmas. Charles Thorsen provided the illustrations, and so it was he who brought the little bear to life. He was by then well known for his work with both Disney and MGM, but his most famous creation was back in 1938 when, during his time with "Merrie" Melodies, he was asked for a cartoon rabbit. He responded by drawing the carrot-chewing Bugs Bunny.

Little Punkinhead may not have found worldwide fame on quite the same scale, but he certainly won the hearts of Canadian children. They loved the story of the bear with the unruly topknot, who was teased by the other bears with their nice smooth heads. He wanted so much to be like them. He tried combing and brushing the errant hair as hard as he could, but it simply sprang straight back up again. He plastered it down with grease, but that didn't help at all, and when his mother cut it for him, it promptly grew back again. Then along came Santa to save the day, and Punkinhead changed from a sad little fellow to one with the broadest of grins.

Many more stories about him followed – a total of 14 in all – and it wasn't long before other Punkinhead merchandise started to appear as well. In due course, Eaton's was selling everything from Punkinhead rugs, lamps and china to slippers, pullovers and towels. There were even Punkinhead doughnuts, and of course it was not long before the store commissioned some soft toy Punkinheads as well.

Shortly after his second appearance in Eaton's Christmas parade in 1948, the new soft toy design was described in the Merrythought Trials Book. "Young bear with top-not of longer pile plush than body," said the entry on 3 January 1949. "Height 16 inches. Inside ears and tummy of lighter plush. Outside ears, head, back body, arms and legs of darker plush. Fawn velveteen muzzle and upper foot. Felt all paw pads. Trousers canary felt. ... Head well rounded. Tummy well out."

This art silk (originally blue) Cheeky has art silk footpads that were originally pink, while the paw pads are pink felt. He is thought to be one of the earliest Cheekys, dating from around 1957.

In fact, in the end, there were three sizes in all – a 10 inch (25.5cm) "baby"; a 16 inch (40.5cm) "large" version; and a 23 inch (58.5cm) giant, said to be suitable for anyone who wanted to give a really big present. All were fully jointed, with a rich brown mohair used as the "darker plush" and a paler shade for the tummy and ear linings. Brown felt was used for the pads, and both red and blue appear to have been more popular colours for the trousers than that original yellow. Green was also apparently available, but again seems to have been less in demand. Large white and black glass eyes were another distinctive feature of the Punkinhead toy.

There were some variations in the mohairs used, but the bears remained basically the same for the seven years or so during which they were produced by Merrythought. The last one was made in 1956 – the year before the first of his descendants, the Merrythought Cheeky, went on sale.

Whereas Punkinhead was sold only in that one Canadian store, the Cheeky was much more widely available, with countless versions appearing over the years. In 1957 alone, he was being made in four sizes – 9 inches (23cm), 11 inches (28cm), 13 inches (33cm) and 15 inches (38cm) – and in two different qualities. The T series was in a rich gold shaggy mohair, while the TAS range was in a "special thick silk plush" (art silk, in other words) in old gold. In addition, there was a PAT series of art silk Cheekys made in the same four sizes but in assorted pastel shades. The following year a giant 25 inch (63.5cm) version was also added to each series, and the 1959 price list noted that music boxes could be added to all bears over 15 inches (38cm).

Made from light gold art silk, this small Cheeky (9 inches/23cm), with the Registered Design label on his foot, dates from the early 1960s.

All were fully jointed and stuffed with kapok to give the softness mentioned by the designer. Bells were inserted in their ears, and would become a trademark of virtually all the Merrythought Cheekys.

Their velveteen muzzles and broad grins were two features that they shared with the earlier Punkinhead. Large ears placed on the side of the head were another factor that both designs had in common, and so were the round felt pads on the (front) paws, but there were also many differences. The Cheeky had no top-knot, for instance, and also no contrasting tum. Conventional amber eyes replaced the distinctive oversized white ones, and there was no velveteen on the upper feet. Initially there were no contrasting ear linings either, although these would be seen in some later versions.

There were a good many later versions. In 1960, for instance, the pastel art silks were replaced by nylon plushes in assorted colours. In 1962 the pastel colours

This Cheeky-style Print Teddy was one of the first Cheekys to be produced in the 1950s, and is today very rare.

Nylon Cheekys were produced in various colours and sizes in the early 1960s; this one also has nylon footpads.

disappeared to be replaced by a new open-mouthed version in honeysuckle nylon, which remained in the catalogue for just one year.

In 1964, a version in "rich London gold shaggy mohair" was added to the existing ones in "rich golden shaggy mohair" and "old gold art silk", and was replaced a year later by one in "Super mohair London gold plush". In 1966, the original "rich golden shaggy mohair" finally disappeared.

It was only in 1969, however, that the old gold art silk was seen for the last time. In 1970 it was replaced by a "Super thick Dark Mink plush", and a new 18 inch (45.5cm) size was added to both the mohair and the "dark mink" series. A year later, the "thick Dark Mink plush" was in turn replaced, this time by a "Simulated Mink" version, which was available in just three sizes – 15 inches (38cm), 18 inches (45.5cm) and 25 inches (63cm).

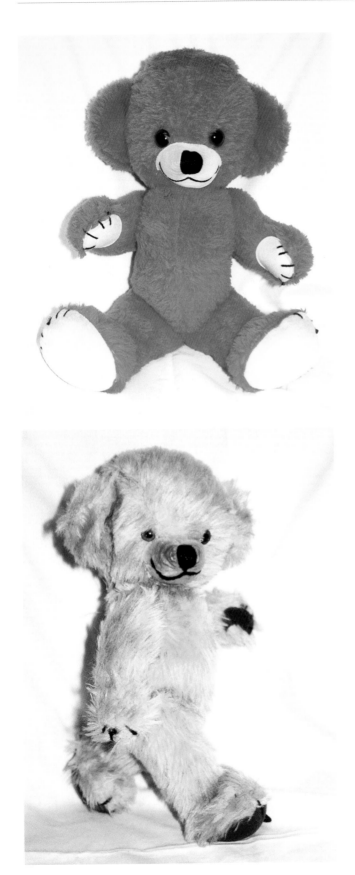

ABOVE:: *An open-mouthed Cheeky in honeysuckle nylon plush was made for just one year (1962).*

ABOVE LEFT: *Cheekys were produced in a number of vibrant colours; this nylon one dates from the early 1960s.*

LEFT: *A rich, golden, shaggy mohair was used for Cheekys in various sizes in the early 1960s.*

ABOVE: *It is rare to find art silk still in its original, shiny state. This bear was bought in the early 1960s and kept packed away for more than three decades.*

ABOVE RIGHT: *Musical versions of some larger Cheekys were available, but are today very rare. This mohair one dates from the late 1960s.*

RIGHT: *This cerise-coloured art silk was one of many shades seen in the 1960s.*

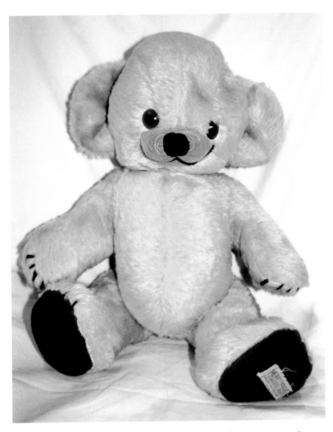

This 1960s mohair Cheeky is very rare, since it has no paw pads.

Brown Dreylon was used for Cheekys in six sizes in 1974.

Simulated mink was used for a range of Cheekys in the 1970s.

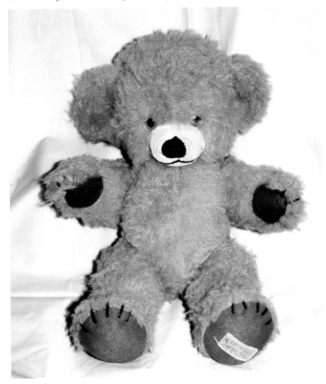

Three years later, in 1974, a "Brown Dreylon" series was added, in the same six sizes as the mohair version, but it would remain in the catalogue for just two years. Both the London Gold mohair and the "Simulated Mink" would remain for the rest of the decade, however, and into the 1980s.

Changes to the design of the catalogue in 1982, and the lack of an accompanying price list in the Merrythought archives, mean that information about that year's range is incomplete. But it appears that the London Gold Cheeky was still available, and had been joined by versions in blue or pink synthetic plush. The following year's catalogue pictured the same three variants, with a price list noting that the Gold was available in 10, 12, 14 and 16 inch sizes (25.5, 30.5, 35.5 and 40.5cm), while the pink and blue were offered only in the 14 inch (35.5cm) size.

Examples made from blue or pink synthetic plush were on sale during the early 1980s.

Pink and blue variants were also on offer in 1984, but each was now in a single 12 inch (30.5cm) size, as was a new "Champagne" Cheeky. A new Golden version, on the other hand, was offered in 10, 12 and 14 inch sizes (25.5, 30.5 and 35.5cm). A year later the colours were given as London Gold, Champagne, Blue and Pink - all in a single 12 inch (30.5cm) size.

Cheeky novelties also appeared from time to time, the first being the 13 inch (33cm) Muff Bear in 1960. Made from pink or blue nylon plush, it had a Cheeky head, with arms and legs hinged on to the muff, which formed the body. Ear linings and foot pads were of white nylon and a squeaker was fitted into the back of the muff itself. A large bow was tied round the bear's neck, and a cord was also attached, so that the muff could be hung round the neck of its owner.

It remained in the catalogue for just two years, but in 1970 a new Muff Bear made its appearance - this time with a mohair head and legs attached to a "mink type

In the mid 1980s a new synthetic plush, with a shorter pile, was used for the blue and pink versions.

The swing tag, shiny foot label, and flock pads help to pinpoint the date of this mohair example to the mid 1980s.

Mr and Mrs Twisty Cheeky were first seen in the 1966 catalogue and remained on sale for three years.

thick plush muff". This version had no arms, but that didn't stop it from remaining on sale for considerably longer than its predecessor. It eventually disappeared in 1976.

A very different kind of Cheeky novelty were Mr and Mrs Twisty Cheeky, who were first seen in the 1966 catalogue as part of the range of Twisty toys. Available in two sizes – 11 inches (28cm) or a 24 inch (61cm) "Showpiece" – they contained a special internal armature which enabled their limbs to be twisted into numerous different positions. Only their heads were of mohair. Their bodies and limbs were made from coloured cloth, topped with removable clothes.

In both cases the body, arms and legs were turquoise, with large black "shoes" and white cloth paws. Over this, Mrs Twisty Cheeky wore a red skirt with a white apron, while her husband sported red trousers and a white collar. Catalogue pictures also show a ribbon around Mr Twisty Cheeky's neck, although this may not have been part of the final version.

The 1977 Bed-time Bear was originally dressed, but this rare surviving example has lost his nightwear.

The Twisty Cheekys appeared only in the 1966, 1967 and 1968 catalogues, and it would be 1977 before another dressed Cheeky was pictured. Known as the Bed-time Bear, and measuring 17 inches (43cm), he took his name from the pyjamas, tartan-lined dressing gown and tartan slippers he was wearing. All the clothes were removable.

The Bed-time Bear remained in the catalogue for just one year, but a number of other Cheeky novelties did not appear in the catalogues at all. A Cheeky glove puppet in "golden plush" was entered in the Trials Book in 1967, for instance, and at least some, in mohair, went on sale. So, too, did large Cheeky nightdress cases in a whole variety of furs, including mohair, art silk, nylon and other synthetics – made for the John Lewis stores. A zip down the bear's back opened to reveal a pocket inside which nightwear could be kept. With the body thus "stuffed",

the bear could be played with in the normal way during the day.

One or two unjointed Cheekys with sewn-in clothing have also come to light, and in the mid 1980s there was a luxury Cheeky in a dense, champagne-coloured plush with a mushroom-coloured plush muzzle instead of the usual velveteen. The same fabric was used for the pads. The furry muzzle hid the usual grin, however, and the bear did not have the typical Cheeky bells in the ears either.

Some London Gold mohair Cheekys continued to be made even when they disappeared from the catalogue in the mid 1980s.

From 1986 onwards, no Cheekys at all were included in the catalogue - although they could still be ordered. It would be the growing interest of collectors that would bring about a huge revival in their fortunes from the early 1990s. Many examples were then included in the International Collectors' Catalogues. Others were made for individual stores or distributors. Details of some of these more recent examples can be found in the chapters covering bears for collectors, and those dealing with specials.

This dressed Cheeky in synthetic plush was bought around 1990, and was not in the catalogue; he may have been a special.

The Classic Cheeky

1957
T: Rich gold shaggy mohair
TAS: Special thick silk plush old gold
PAT: Quality as TAS but assorted pastel colours
All in 9 inch (23cm), 11 inch (28cm), 13 inch (33cm) and 15 inch (38cm) sizes

1958, 1959
T: Rich gold shaggy mohair
TAS: Thick old gold silk plush
PAT: Assorted pastel colours, thick silk plush
All in 9 inch (23cm), 11 inch (28cm), 13 inch (33cm), 15 inch (38cm) and 25 inch (63.5cm) sizes

1960, 1961
T: Rich gold shaggy mohair
TAS: Thick old gold silk plush
TNY: Assorted pastel colours, nylon plush
All in 9 inch (23cm), 11 inch (28cm), 13 inch (33cm), 15 inch (38cm) and 25 inch (63.5cm) sizes
Music boxes could be added to all bears over 15 inches

1962
T: Rich golden shaggy mohair
TAS: Thick old gold silk plush
O: Open-mouth version in honeysuckle nylon plush
All in 9 inch (23cm), 11 inch (28cm), 13 inch (33cm), 15 inch (38cm) and 25 inch (63.5cm) sizes

1963
T: Rich golden shaggy mohair
TAS: Thick old gold silk plush
Both in 9 inch (23cm), 11 inch (28cm), 13 inch (33cm), 15 inch (38cm) and 25 inch (63.5cm) sizes

1964
T: Rich golden shaggy mohair
LLT: Rich London gold shaggy mohair
TAS: Thick old gold silk plush
All in 9 inch (23cm), 11 inch (28cm), 13 inch (33cm), 15 inch (38cm) and 25 inch (63.5cm) sizes

1965
T: Rich golden shaggy mohair
TAS: Close rich pile old gold silk plush
G.T: Super mohair London gold plush
All in 9 inch (23cm), 11 inch (28cm), 13 inch (33cm), 15 inch (38cm) and 25 inch (63.5cm) sizes

1966, 1967
TAS: Close rich pile old gold silk plush
G.T: Super mohair London gold plush
Both in 9 inch (23cm), 11 inch (28cm), 13 inch (33cm), 15 inch (38cm) and 25 inch (63.5cm) sizes

1968
TAS: Art silk plush in an attractive shade of Old Gold
GT: Best quality mohair in rich Gold
Both in 9 inch (23cm), 11 inch (28cm), 13 inch (33cm), 15 inch (38cm) and 25 inch (63.5cm) sizes

1969
TAS: Art silk plush in an attractive shade of Old Gold
GT: Best quality mohair in rich Gold
Both in 9 inch (23cm), 11 inch (28cm), 13 inch (33cm), 15 inch (38cm) and 25 inch (63.5cm) sizes

1970
GT: Best quality hard wearing mohair plush
BT: Super thick Dark Mink plush
Both in 9 inch (23cm), 11 inch (28cm), 13 inch (33cm), 15 inch (38cm), 18 inch (45.5cm) and 25 inch (63.5cm) sizes

1971, 1972, 1973
GT: Best quality mohair
Sizes: 9 inches (23cm), 11 inches (28cm), 13 inches (33cm), 15 inches (38cm), 18 inches (45.5cm) and 25 inches (63.5cm)

CT: Simulated Mink
Sizes: 15 inches (38cm), 18 inches (45.5cm), 25 inches (63.5cm)

1974, 1975
GT: London gold mohair
Sizes: 9 inches (23cm), 11 inches (28cm), 13 inches (33cm), 15 inches (38cm), 18 inches (45.5cm) and 25 inches (63.5cm)

CT: Simulated Mink
Sizes: 15 inches (38cm), 18 inches (45.5cm), 25 inches (63.5cm)

TNY: Brown Dreylon
Sizes: 9 inches (23cm), 11 inches (28cm), 13 inches (33cm), 15 inches (38cm), 18 inches (45.5cm) and 25 inches (63.5cm)

1976, 1977, 1978, 1979
GT: London gold mohair
Sizes: 9 inches (23cm), 11 inches (28cm), 13 inches (33cm), 15 inches (38cm), 18 inches (45.5cm) and 25 inches (63.5cm)

CT: Simulated Mink
Sizes: 15 inches (38cm), 18 inches (45.5cm), 25 inches (63.5cm)

1980
GT: London gold mohair blend
Sizes: 9 inches (23cm), 11 inches (28cm), 13 inches (33cm), 15 inches (38cm), 18 inches (45.5cm) and 25 inches (63.5cm)

CT: Simulated Mink
Sizes: 15 inches (38cm), 18 inches (45.5cm), 25 inches (63.5cm)

1981
GT: London gold mohair blend
Sizes: 9 inches (23cm), 11 inches (28cm), 13 inches (33cm), 15 inches (38cm), 18 inches (45.5cm) and 25 inches (63.5cm)

CT: Simulated Mink
Sizes: 13 inches (33cm), 15 inches (38cm), 18 inches (45.5cm), 25 inches (63.5cm)

1982
The catalogue gives only codes GT, BLT and PKT for Gold, Pink and Blue, with no further details, and there is no price list in the Merrythought archives.

1983
GT: Gold mohair
Sizes: 10 inches (25.5 cm), 12 inches (30.5cm), 14 inches (35.5cm) and 16 inches (40.5cm)

PKT: Pink plush
BLT: Blue plush
Both in 14 inch (35.5cm) size

1984
PT (given as PKT in price list): Pink plush
BT (given as BLT in price list): Blue plush
(NEW) LT: Champagne
All in 12 inch (30.5cm) size
(NEW) MT: Golden
Sizes: 10 inches (25.5cm), 12 inches (30.5cm), 14 inches (35.5cm)

1985
M: London Gold
L: Champagne
B: Blue
P: Pink
All in 12 inch (30.5cm) size

Chapter 9

9. THE 1990s ONWARDS: THE TOY CATALOGUES

1990

In 1990, Merrythought celebrated its Diamond Jubilee, but much of that year's catalogue was very similar to that of the previous year. There was, however, one very notable exception: on the front cover was a picture of the first limited-edition to go on sale worldwide. The Diamond Jubilee Bear proved to be a huge success, with all 2,500 quickly sold out.

A year later, Merrythought introduced the first of its special International Collectors' Catalogues – filled entirely with items designed to appeal to the more serious collectors. The range of children's soft toys – including teddies – remained as wide as ever, however, and from 1991 onwards these had their own separate catalogue.

Meanwhile, in the Jubilee Year itself, things continued very much as before, with even the layout of the catalogue remarkably similar to that of the previous year, and with many old favourites still included among the bears.

The jointed London Gold bears were unchanged, for instance, and still available in both mohair and synthetic plushes – in the same range of sizes as before. The 18

The 1990 Bedtime Bear was a fully jointed ted, made from synthetic plush, and measuring 14 inches (35.5cm).

inch (45.5cm) was still also available in a musical version or with a growl, with the bears wearing bibs stating "I play a tune" or "I growl", respectively.

The Butterscotch and Nutmeg Bears had not been altered either. Both were made in synthetic plush – the Butterscotch version again in 13, 17, 21 and 26 inch sizes (33, 43, 53.5 and 66cm), and the Nutmeg one, with his plastic nose, measuring 18, 22 or 26 inches (45.5, 56 or 66cm). In addition, there was a new, gold, 14 inch (35.5cm) Bedtime Bear made from synthetic plush – in the same design as the jointed London Gold Bear, but wearing a multi-coloured, striped nightshirt and matching cap.

The 5-inch (12.5cm) London Gold Miniature Bear, in short-pile mohair, was unchanged as well, and so were the 10 inch (25.5cm) Ironbridge Bears, available in black, fawn and silver-grey synthetic plushes as well as London Gold mohair. The four Dressed Bears (Beefeater, Highland Bear, Guardsman and London Policeman) had been retained as well, although in each case the 36 inch (91.5cm) versions had been discontinued, leaving just two sizes, namely 18 inches (45.5cm) and 78 inches (nearly 2 metres).

These London Gold mohair bears were available in eight sizes, with growling or musical versions of the 18 inch (45.5cm) version.

There were four versions of the fully jointed Ironbridge Bear in the 1990 catalogue; only that in London Gold (shown on the left) was made from mohair.

There was also a new dressed Father Christmas Bear, wearing a traditional white-trimmed red coat and hat. He was a different design from the other dressed bears, however, being unjointed and with head and paws made from gold synthetic plush. He also had a seam running down the centre of his face, rather than the more conventional inset muzzle, and a triangular nose instead of the rather squarish style (with elongated outer stitches) seen on the other dressed bears. The sizes were different too – namely 16 and 24 inches (40.5 and 61cm).

Other items that also remained on sale included the 10 inch (25.5cm) sitting Tickle Tummie Panda and Tickle

The Beefeater, Policeman and Guardsman Glove Puppets were all seen for the first time in 1990 and remained in the catalogue until 1998.

Tummie Bear – the latter made from cream plush with a lighter coloured tummy and with heat-sealed detailing on his pads. Also still available were the colourful Clown Teddy Bear nightdress case, with his red and blue body, and the Sailor Bear Nightdress Case in his blue uniform, as well as the Muff and Purse Bear. The Bear Glove Puppet remained, too – but he had been joined by Policeman, Beefeater and Guardsman puppets, all of which again measured 10 inches (25.5cm).

The Teddy Bear Brooch and china beaker had likewise been retained. But the bear-decorated Christmas stocking had gone, along with the Bungie Bear and the Polar Bear Cuddle Cub, and there was a new cuddly panda on all fours, made from synthetic plush and measuring 15 inches (38cm). There was also a new Miniature (4 inch/10cm) Teddy Bear Muff, and a Miniature Teddy Bear Backpack (8 inches/20.5cm) – both ideal as accessories for larger bears.

A number of supplementary lines were added to the range later in the year. They included two bears. One was the cuddly, unjointed Snuggle Bear in a fairly long-pile, cream plush, made in 14 and 32 inch versions (35.5 and 81cm). The other was a Sitting Polar Bear, produced in 9 and 18 inch sizes (23 and 45.5cm), with the latter also available as a nightdress case.

Many of the bears from the 1990 catalogue remained on sale the following year as well – with most of them in the soft toy catalogue rather than that for collectors. But the London Gold Miniature Bear, the Miniature Muff and Miniature Back Pack had been moved to the International Collectors' Catalogue, along with the beaker and brooch.

Unchanged among the toy teds were the London Gold Bears (in both mohair and synthetic plush), which were still available in the same wide range of sizes. The Butterscotch and Nutmeg Bears remained the same as well, as did the Bedtime Bear in his stripy nightshirt and cap, the four Ironbridge Bears, the Tickle Tummie Bear and Panda, the Clown and Sailor Bear nightdress cases, the Muff and Purse Bear, and the four Bear Glove Puppets.

The London Policeman Bear (left) and the Highland Bear (right) were joined in 1991 by the new Chelsea Pensioner Bear (centre).

In 1991, an Airline Pilot Bear (left) and a John Bull Bear (right) joined the popular Guardsman Bear (centre) in the Heritage Collection of dressed bears.

There were many changes, however, including a large number of new arrivals. A range of dressed bears was still on offer, for example, and they still included a Beefeater, Guardsman, London Policeman and Highland Bear. But they were in a new, unjointed design and the mohair had been replaced by synthetic plush, which was used for the heads, paws and feet; the clothing still formed the bodies and limbs.

The range had also been expanded into a whole Heritage Collection, with the addition of an Airline Pilot, Fighter Pilot, Graduate, Golfer, Cricketer, Chelsea Pensioner and John Bull Bear. The Beefeater, Guardsman, London Policeman and Highland Bear were all offered in both 16 and 78 inch sizes (40.5cm and nearly 2 metres),

while the remainder were available only in the smaller version.

The Father Christmas Bear had gone, as had the Snuggle Bear and the Panda on all fours, but in their place were new Sitting Pandas in three sizes (10, 15 and 32 inches/25.5, 38 and 81cm) and a 12 inch (30.5cm) Koala. A Sitting Polar Bear measuring 12 inches (30.5cm) replaced the 9 inch (23cm) version that had been one of the 1990 supplementary lines, but the 18 inch (45.5cm)

Graduate and Fighter Pilot Bears were among the new arrivals when the range of dressed bears was expanded into a comprehensive Heritage Collection in 1991.

Although only two of the new Sitting Pandas were illustrated in the 1991 catalogue, they were actually available in three sizes.

The larger of these two Sitting Polar Bears, measuring 18 inches (45.5cm), was introduced in 1990, while the 12 inch (30.5cm) size was first seen the following year.

version remained unchanged – as did the nightdress case in the same size.

There were several new nightdress cases as well – including a 12 inch (30.5cm) Tickle Tummie Bear and a 15 inch (38cm) Sitting Panda. In addition, 20 inch (51cm) Beefeater and Guardsman Bear nightdress cases were introduced, with head and paws made from synthetic plush and with their clothes forming the sachets.

White T-shirts decorated with a Merrythought bear also went on sale – in three sizes for children and three for adults – but they had disappeared by the following year, which again saw many changes, although a number of old favourites were retained.

Still included, for example, were the London Gold bears in mohair and synthetic plush, in the same range of sizes – although the bibs on the musical and growling versions had been replaced by rectangular tags. The 14 inch (35.5cm) size was also still available dressed in his nightshirt and cap.

The four Ironbridge Bears were there as well, along with the Nutmeg Bear in his three sizes. But the Butterscotch ones had given way to a new Chocolate Bear, with a longer snout and made from a brown synthetic plush. His pads were in contrasting oyster (pale cream) plush, and he was made in four sizes – 14, 17, 21 and 26 inches (35.5, 43, 53.5 and 66cm).

Also new was the unjointed Snuggles, made from a shaggy plush in three sizes – 18, 26 and 36 inches (45.5, 66 and 91.5cm), while the Tickle Tummie Bear had been replaced by a redesigned Tickle Tum Bear, measuring 15 inches (38cm) and again made in a creamy plush with a lighter tummy. Like his predecessor, he was in a permanently sitting pose, but the detailing on the pads was now airbrushed.

The unjointed Snuggles, made from a shaggy plush, was a new arrival in 1992 and was available in a total of three sizes.

Claws were airbrushed on to the footpads of the cuddly new Do Not Disturb Bear, which was made from a creamy plush with a white tummy. Measuring 18 inches (45.5cm), she was in a sitting position, and carried a sleeping baby bear in her arms.

The Tickle Tummie Panda and the Sitting Panda in three sizes had also been replaced – by a fully jointed panda, measuring 14 inches (35.5cm), and the pair of Sitting Polar Bears gave way to a snow white, 14 inch (35.5cm) cuddly Snowy Polar Bear on all fours. The koala, on the other hand, remained unchanged.

In 1992, Merrythought added a new, jointed panda to its range of toys; it measured 14 inches (35.5cm) and was made from a synthetic plush.

There were also relatively few changes to the Heritage Collection, apart from the disappearance of the Airline and Fighter Pilots, and the addition of a 78 inch (nearly 2 metres) version of the Chelsea Pensioner. But a new arrival was a 15 inch Clown Bear, whose two-colour body was similar in design to that of the Clown nightdress case, but this time in aqua and lilac. The head had been totally redesigned, however, and the new bear measured just 15 inches (38cm).

There were changes among the novelty items as well. The four Glove Puppet Bears remained the same,

but the Muff and Purse Bear – with gold plush head, paws and feet attached to the muff body – had been replaced by a totally different design. A brightly coloured muff, which also incorporated a zipped purse, was simply decorated with a plush bear's head, with a tartan bow at the neck.

A 12 inch (30.5cm) Cushion Nightwear Case Bear was similar to the muff, but there was also a new Bedtime Clown nightdress case – similar in design to the previous clown nightdress case, but with the red and blue body replaced by red and yellow. Like his predecessor, he measured 21 inches (53.5cm), and there was a smaller, 15 inch (38cm) Clown Sachet, featuring a head in the same design as the new 1992 Clown Bear, but this time with a red and yellow body.

The Bedtime Beefeater and Bedtime Guardsman nightdress cases were the same as the Beefeater and Guardsman Bears introduced the previous year. But the Sitting Panda, Sitting Polar Bear and Tickle Tummie Bear cases had gone, to be replaced by a 15 inch (38cm) Tickle Tum Bear and an 18 inch (45.5cm) Do Not Disturb Bear. Both of these nightdress cases were similar in design to the regular soft toys of the same names. There was also a new Sleep Tight Bear, made from a creamy plush with a blue shirt – intended to be just the right size to hold a hot water bottle.

A similar combination of brand-new teds and old favourites appeared in the catalogue for the following year, 1993, when one of the most notable changes was the absence of the London Gold Bear in synthetic plush. The mohair version remained, however – in the familiar range of sizes, but with the musical and growling versions of the 18 inch (45.5cm) size wearing deep red bows that carried the words "I play a tune" or "I Growl."

Both the Chocolate Bear and the Nutmeg Bear had also gone, with their place being taken by the new Classic Teddy Bears. Again fully jointed and made in a brown synthetic plush – lighter in colour than that of the Chocolate Bear – he was in the same design as the London Gold Bear made from mohair, and available in the same nine sizes as the missing plush version had been. Once more there were musical and growling variants of the 18 inch (45.5cm) size, wearing the same bows as the musical and growling versions of the mohair London Gold Bear.

A new range of Classic Teddy Bears – fully jointed and made from synthetic plush – was introduced in 1993, and was available in nine sizes.

Another new jointed range was the Brown Sugar Bears, made from a fudge-coloured, frosted plush. They were offered in four sizes (21, 26, 32 and 40 inches/53.5, 66, 81 and 101.5cm).

There was a new chocolate-coloured Ironbridge Bear as well – joining the existing four in the soft toy range.

The 1993 Brown Sugar Bears were made from a fudge-coloured frosted plush, in a total of four sizes.

Snuggles was given new plush and a new bow, and was joined by three similarly unjointed Truffles Bean Belly Bears, measuring 14, 18 and 32 inches (35.5, 45.5 and 81cm). Made from brown synthetic plush, with white plush pads and ear linings, they were given bean-filled tums to make them sit fetchingly.

Also totally new were four cuddly, 12 inch (30.5cm), dressed bears inspired by well-known nursery rhymes. Little Miss Muffet wore a yellow dress with white cap and apron. Old King Cole was given a red one-piece suit and gold cloth crown. Little Bo Beep was dressed in a pretty green and floral print dress and bonnet, while Wee Willie Winkie sported a white nightshirt, with blue and white striped collar and cuffs that matched his striped nightcap.

The dressed Beefeater, Guardsman, Policeman and Highland Bear in the Heritage Collection, on the other hand, were old favourites. But they had been joined by a new Sherlock Holmes bear in 18 and 78 inch sizes (45.5cm and nearly 2 metres), as well as a nurse (16

(Left to right) Little Miss Muffet, Wee Willie Winkie, Old King Cole and Little Bo Beep were all new in 1993.

inches/40.5cm) and a Happy Hobo in patched suit and tall, battered hat (16 and 78 inches/40.5cm and nearly 2 metres). They replaced the Golfer, Cricketer, Graduate, Chelsea Pensioner and John Bull Bears, which were all missing from the 1993 range.

Also missing were the Clown Bear and the Jointed Panda, and there was a new grey colour for the Koala Bear. But the Tickle Tum Bear and the Do Not Disturb Bear remained, as did the Snowy Polar Bear, and there was also a return of the Cuddle Cub Bear, Panda and Polar Bear (although there had been some modifications to the designs since the 1980s versions). The 1993 examples were included in a special Wildlife Showcase, and were all produced in 24 and 36 inch sizes (61 and 91.5cm).

Many of the novelty bear items were also the same as those on sale the previous year – among them the four glove puppets and the muff with purse. But there were a number of changes among the nighttime designs. The Sleep Tight hot water bottle cover had gone, and so had the Cushion Nightwear Case, along with the Bedtime Beefeater and the Bedtime Guardsman. But the two Clowns remained, as did the Tickle Tum Bear and the Do Not Disturb Bear nightdress cases, and there was a

The 1993 Cuddle Cub Bears were both sizable toys - measuring 24 and 36 inches (61 and 91.5cm) - and were part of a special Wildlife Showcase.

cuddly new Snuggles case, measuring 26 inches (66cm). A Pampered Bears sachet, featuring two bears' heads peeping out over the top of a blue quilted "bed", also went on sale.

107

Bears continued to feature heavily in the 1994 soft toy catalogue, which again included some classic, fully jointed bears in both mohair and synthetic plush, as well as a wide variety of cuddlies. The London Gold Teddy Bears in pure mohair were still one of the mainstays of the range, and a new 10 inch (25.5cm) size was added, making a total of nine sizes in all. But there was also a brand-new ted that was clearly intended for children but was made from a high-quality mohair. Known as James Bear, he was distinctly superior-looking, and was available in 15 and 21 inch sizes (38 and 53.5cm).

Peter and Pippa (1994) were unjointed, cuddly teddies, made from synthetic plush and with clothing in a strawberry print fabric.

The 1994 James was a fully jointed, mohair bear and was available in two sizes.

As in previous years, there was another fully jointed mohair version of the Ironbridge Bear, which was offered in the same five colours as the previous year. The remaining four were in synthetic plush, as were the Classic Teddy Bears and the Brown Sugar Bears. Both had also been on sale in 1993, but the Classic Bears were now changed to a new toffee colour.

The Truffles Bean Belly bears returned as well, while a new variant of Snuggles was produced. He was in a warm treacle colour with beige pads and ear linings, and was given the new name Hugabear. Like his predecessor, he was available in 18, 26 and 36 inch sizes (45.5, 66 and 91.5cm).

There were also two totally new cuddlies, carrying the names Peter and Pippa. Unjointed and made from a gold synthetic plush, they both measured 11 inches (28cm) in height. Peter wore a red bow tie with a

waistcoat made from a strawberry print fabric, while Pippa was given a dress in the same cloth. They replaced the previous year's four "nursery rhyme" bears.

There were replacements, too, for the Happy Hobo in the Heritage Collection, who made way for Charlie Chop, the butcher, and for Robin Hood. The others all remained, although Sherlock Holmes was pictured in a brighter outfit, made from checked cloth, instead of the mottled fabric of the previous year.

The Tickle Tum Bear, the three Cuddle Cubs (each in two sizes) and the Koala all remained in the range as well, but in 1994 the only Do Not Disturb Bear was that in the form of a nightdress case. The Tickle Tum Bear and Pampered Bears nightwear cases were still available as well, although the two Clowns were no longer in the catalogue, and the Snuggles nightdress case had been replaced by the new Hugabear.

Other changes included the disappearance of the Muff with Purse. Instead, there was a return of the Traditional Bear Muff, in which a plush head, paws and feet were attached to a muff "body". There was also a new novelty Bedroom Tidy, with a bear's head and with outstretched arms on which a child's clothes could be hung. But the four Glove Puppet Bears were old favourites, and still included the Beefeater, Policeman and Guardsman.

In 1995, the soft toy catalogue again included a fully jointed mohair bear – replacing the previous year's James, and in a similar style to him. Known as The Laird, he was snowy white with striking tartan paw pads, and was offered in the same two sizes as his predecessor, namely 15 and 21 inches (38 and 53.5cm).

A new London Gold plush was used for the Classic Bears in 1995, and they remained in the range in 1996.

The mohair London Gold Teddy Bears remained as well, in the same range of sizes. But there was a new gold synthetic plush for the Classic Bears, although there was no change to the sizes, and the 18 inch (45.5cm) version was still available with a growl or music box, and wearing a bow confirming that fact.

Another fully jointed range, the Brown Sugar Bears, had been discontinued, however, and their place taken by four Toffee Twist Bears in a beautifully soft, mock Persian lamb fabric. The only change to the Ironbridge Bears, on the other hand, was the disappearance of the silver-grey version.

The catalogue also included a totally new selection of unjointed cuddlies. The previous year's Peter and Pippa had disappeared, along with the Hugabears and the Truffles Bean Belly bears. In their place were the ultra-huggable Cosy Bears, made from a long-pile plush in a pale fudge colour with silvery tips, and in 14, 18 and 32 inch sizes (35.5, 45.5 and 81 cm). Their cousins, the brown Calvin Bears, measured 18 and 24 inches (45.5 and 61cm), while another new offering was a 15 inch (38cm), unjointed, black bear by the name of Arthur.

Once again, there were changes to the dressed Heritage Collection as well, with Robin Hood, the Nurse and Charlie Chop disappearing to make way for three new designs, all measuring 16 inches (40.5cm). Jack Tar wore a suitably nautical, blue and white striped, sewn-in jumper and dark blue, sewn-in trousers, with a blue and white HMS Merrythought cap. The Duchess was regal in a long blue dress trimmed with black, and with matching

hat, while the third new arrival was a tartan-clad Piper Bear, complete with bagpipes. He was the perfect companion for the Highland Bear – a long-time favourite that remained in the range along with the Beefeater, Guardsman, London Policeman and Sherlock Holmes.

The Cuddle Cub Bear, Panda and Polar Bear were other old favourites making another appearance, and the four glove puppets were likewise included in the range once more. But there was a new design for the Koala (again measuring 10 inches/25.5cm), and the Kiddies Corner included a new Tinkle Bear for young babies, that jingled merrily when shaken. White in colour, she wore a yellow sewn-in dress, with the mechanism concealed inside the skirt.

The Traditional Muff, on the other hand, was another of the already-familiar faces, as was the Bedroom Tidy Bear, while the nightwear cases included the Tickle Tum Bear and the Do Not Disturb mother and baby. The Pampered Bears sachet was also retained, but the Hugabear case was replaced by new Cosy Bear and Calvin Bear designs in the same size of 18 inches (45.5cm).

In 1996, there was no brand-new, fully jointed, mohair bear as there had been in the previous two years. The popular London Gold mohair range was still there, though, as were the Classic Bears, and a new mohair version of the Ironbridge Bear, this time a coffee-coloured one, joined that in London Gold.

The only other jointed bears were the black and chocolate-coloured Ironbridge Bears in synthetic plush

The Champagne Bear, made from a synthetic plush in three sizes, was among the new arrivals in 1996.

(the fawn was no longer shown) and a new Champagne Bear, made from a champagne-coloured, synthetic plush in 18, 21 and 26 inch sizes (45.5, 53.5 and 66cm).

There were, on the other hand, several brand-new, unjointed cuddlies. Among them were the soft and huggable Comfy Bears that came in three sizes – two of them (15 and 20 inches/38 and 51cm) small enough to be cuddled and the largest (40 inches/101.5cm) big enough to do the cuddling! They were available in white or rust.

Also new was the equally cuddly Bubble Brown Bear, made from a dark brown plush with silver tips in 22 and 33 inch sizes (56 and 84cm), while the Squeak Beige Bear was of a similar design but took his name from the colour of his fur and the squeaker contained inside him.

The Bubble Brown Bears were cuddly new additions to the range in 1996.

Two small, unjointed 7 inch (18cm) teddies were also introduced. The Girl Soft Bear was made in a creamy fabric, with a blue print cloth used for her paw pads and large collar. The Boy Soft Bear was slightly darker, with plain blue pads matching his bow tie.

The only new thing about the Cuddle Cubs, on the other hand, was that the brown bear had been discontinued, leaving only the Polar Bear and the Panda. And in the Heritage Collection, the Duchess and the Piper Bear had both disappeared after only one year, although the Jack Tar remained. In their place were two more new arrivals – this time a one-armed Nelson Bear

and another wearing the uniform of the Household Cavalry. Nelson Bear was made in just a single, 16 inch (40.5cm) size, but there were three versions of the Household Cavalry Bear, measuring 16, 36 and 78 inches (40.5cm, 91.5cm and nearly 2 metres).

There was another Koala as well – still in the same 10 inch (25.5cm) size – but the four Glove Puppet bears remained the same, although there were many changes among the other novelty items. The previous year's Tinkle Bear had been dropped, for example, and the Bedroom Tidy Bear had been joined by a brand-new Beefeater version, complete with Beefeater's hat. A set of three bears in different colours was also included in a new range of Merrythought golf club covers (the others were dogs and frogs).

The teddy nightwear cases were changed completely from those of the previous year. Gone were the Do Not Disturb and Tickle Tum Bear versions, along with the Cosy Bear, the Calvin Bear and the Pampered Bears. In their place were Bedtime Comfy Bears – nightwear-case versions of the 20 inch (51cm) rust or white Comfy Bears toys – while the Cuddle Cub Polar Bear and Panda also appeared in nightdress-case form.

The 1996 Bedtime Comfy Bears were nightdress case versions of the Comfy Bears that were introduced at the same time.

The most striking aspect of the next year's soft toy catalogue (1997) was the introduction of a brand-new, fully jointed ted in a wide range of sizes. Known as the Shropshire Bear, he was made in a luxurious gold mohair as well as in a brown synthetic plush. The Shropshire Pure Mohair Bear was available in six sizes – 10, 12, 14, 16, 20 and 26 inches (25.5, 30.5, 35.5, 40.5, 51 and 66cm)

The 1997 Shropshire Bears were available in a wide range of sizes, and there was a mohair version, seen here, as well as one in synthetic plush.

– while the Shropshire Classic Bear in synthetic plush was made only in the four largest sizes.

In both cases, the 16 inch (40.5cm) size could be fitted with a growl or a musical movement, in which case the 'I growl' or 'I play a tune' bows were added – just as they were in the case of the 18 inch (45.5cm) mohair London Gold Teddy Bears, which remained in the range in the usual nine sizes.

The previous year's four Ironbridge Bears (two of them in mohair) remained in the catalogue as well. But they were joined by a new Ironbridge Autumn Bear, made from a sparse, caramel-coloured mohair, and offered in no fewer than six sizes (8, 10, 13, 15, 17 and 20 inches/20.5, 25.5, 33, 38, 43 and 51cm).

A number of other designs had disappeared. All nine sizes of the Classic Bears in gold plush had been discontinued, for example, along with the three jointed Champagne Bears, the Cuddle Cubs Polar Bears and Pandas, and the sitting Squeak Beige Bear in both sizes. But both the white and the rust Comfy Bears remained, along with the Bubbles Brown Bear, which was joined by a similar Brandy Bear in the same sizes but a different, hedgehog brown synthetic plush.

As usual, there were a few changes to the Heritage Bears as well, with Jack Tar and Sherlock Holmes absent

but a new 16 inch (40.5cm) Chef Bear in their place. The Koala was likewise missing from the 1997 range, but a new 20 inch (51cm) Comfy Panda was introduced – as huggable as the bears of the same name.

There was a nightwear case version of this panda as well, to go with the Bedtime Comfy Bears nightwear cases introduced the previous year. But the Cuddle Cub cases were no longer to be seen. Other novelty items remained, however – namely the four Glove Puppet bears, the Golf Club Covers and the two Bedroom Tidy Bears – and they were joined by four little Logo Bears, measuring just 7 inches (18cm). Offered in a choice of red, pink, lemon or white, they could be adorned with ribbons carrying any name – the idea being that they could be used as promotional bears by shops, charities or companies.

Presumably they failed to catch on, as they remained in the catalogue for just a year. The Shropshire Bears in brown synthetic plush disappeared equally quickly, as did the Ironbridge Autumn Bears – although in each case there was a new bear in the same design and the same range of sizes in 1998, but made from a different fabric. A honey-coloured plush was used for the four Honeycomb Classic Bears, for example – made in the same four sizes as the Shropshire Classic Bears of the previous year. The Ironbridge Barley Bear, on the other hand, took his name from the colour of the mohair used for his fur and was made in the same six sizes as the Ironbridge Autumn Bears had been.

There were some new shades among the smaller 10 inch (25.5cm) Ironbridge Bears as well. Those in gold mohair and black synthetic plush remained, but the chocolate-coloured version and that made from coffee-coloured mohair were gone – and in their place were versions in Honey, Nutmeg, Caramel and Baroque Gold synthetic plush.

Among the other new bears in synthetic plush was Topsy – a cuddly teddy in a pale honey colour and with illusion joints, made in four sizes (16, 20, 24 and 48 inches/40.5, 51, 61 and 122cm). The 20 inch (51cm), fully jointed Cookie, on the other hand, was a rich rust colour, with flock pile pads and matching ear linings. The white and rust Comfy Bears, however, were no longer to be seen. Nor were the Bubbles Brown Bears, although Brandy Bear remained unchanged.

The 1998 Topsy was available in four sizes and was made from a synthetic plush.

The bears in the Heritage Collection also remained, and were joined by a new Fireman Bear in 16, 36 and 78 inch sizes (40.5cm, 91.5cm and nearly 2 metres). But the Comfy Panda had been superseded by a new 14 inch (35.5cm) sitting one, which was again also made in a nightcase version.

There was a 16 inch (40.5cm) nightcase version of the new Topsy as well, known as Bedtime Topsy, but the Bedtime Comfy Bears and Panda were among the toys no longer to be found. Gone, too, were the Golf Club Covers – but the four teddy Glove Puppets and the two Bedroom Tidy Bears appeared yet again.

All the puppets and the Beefeater Bedroom Tidy were, however, absent from the 1999 catalogue, which saw many other changes. The pure mohair London Gold

Teddy Bears were still there, as were the mohair Shropshire Bears - both in their usual range of sizes, including the musical and growling versions. But the Shropshire Bears in synthetic plush were no longer to be found.

A new Ironbridge Shortcake bear in a pale biscuit-coloured synthetic plush took the place of the 1998 Ironbridge Barley Bear, made from mohair. Again it was offered in six sizes, ranging from 8 inches to 20 inches (20.5cm to 51cm), but for the first time the 15 inch (38cm) size was also available with either a growl or a musical movement. Of the 10 inch (25.5cm) Ironbridge Bears, the Honey and Caramel versions were missing. In their place was a new Ironbridge Cream Bear in a shaggy mohair.

Cookie made another appearance, but was joined by the silvery grey Pewter – also fully jointed, and measuring 16 inches (40.5cm). Topsy, too, remained unchanged but the cuddly, sitting Brandy Bear was no

The fully jointed Cookie (standing) was among the new arrivals in 1998, while Pewter joined the range a year later.

A new Toy Chest Bear joined the range in 1999; he was made from a luxurious synthetic plush, with a print fabric for his pads and bow tie.

longer on offer. There was, however, a new Toy Chest Bear – made in a beautifully soft, champagne-coloured synthetic plush, with his pads and bow tie made from a colourful print fabric featuring typical toy chest contents. He had illusion joints, like Topsy, and he was made in two sizes – 15 and 18 inches (38 and 45.5cm).

A more noteworthy change in 1999 was a total redesign of the bears in the Heritage Collection. The massive Showpiece versions, measuring 78 inches (nearly 2 metres), were unaltered, apart from the addition of a new Welsh Lady Bear. But the smaller sizes were no longer standing bears, as they had been since their introduction. Instead, they were cuddly, sitting teddies –

In 1999, sitting versions of some of the Heritage Collection bears were introduced – among them the Guardsman.

each of them offered in 12, 21 and 32 inch sizes (30.5, 53.5 and 81cm). There were seven in the range – among them new versions of the ever-popular Guardsman, Beefeater, Policeman, Household Cavalry and Highland Bears, as well as a Welsh Lady Bear and a Country Squire.

The sitting Panda, on the other hand, remained unchanged, although the nightdress case version was no

The 1999 Glove You animals were at the same time both cuddly toys and glove puppets, and included a bear.

longer in the range. The Bedtime Topsy nightcase was still included, though, and a new Panda Bedroom Tidy joined the Bear one. A teddy was also to be found among the new, softly stuffed, Glove You range, which were designed to be both cuddly toys and glove puppets.

Like all the other bears and animals in the soft toy catalogue, they were intended to be played with – but, since 1991, Merrythought had also been publishing a special catalogue containing non-toy bears, for collectors. For the year 2000, the two publications were combined in a single volume for the first time.

Once again, though, there were plenty of bears among all the soft toys. The traditional London Gold Bears, made from mohair, were still on offer in the same nine sizes as before – with musical and growling versions of the 18 inch (45.5cm) size. Alongside them were some "Traditional Style Growler Bears", in the eight larger sizes, made from a honey-coloured synthetic plush. The Ironbridge Shortcake bears were still there too, in the same range of sizes as before, and again with the musical and growling versions in the 15 inch (38cm) size. The Ironbridge Black, Gold Mohair, Nutmeg and Cream Bears were all available as well, although the Baroque Gold version had gone and his place had been taken by new Silver and Sand Stone examples.

The previous year's Toy Chest Bears remained in the new catalogue too, and so did Topsy – in the same four sizes, and with the nightcase version as well. The Glove You bear (Glove You Little Sweetie) was also there, along with the Bear and Panda Bedroom Tidies, but the Shropshire Bears had gone, as had Pewter and Cookie, and the standing Heritage Bears were back in the place of the previous year's sitting ones. In the range were Beefeater, Guardsman, Policeman, Highland, Chef, Household Cavalry, Fireman, Traffic Warden and Oxford Don Bears – all available in 16, 36 and 78 inch versions (40.5cm, 91.5cm and near 2 metres).

Two totally new designs, on the other hand, were a cuddly sitting koala (12 inches/30.5cm) and a slightly larger sitting panda (14 inches/35.5cm). They could be found again in the 2001 catalogue – which again combined both toys and collectors' items in a single publication.

Other familiar designs that year included the traditional London Gold Teddy Bears, the Honey Growler Bears, the various Ironbridge Bears, the Toy Chest Bears and Topsy – all in the same variations as the previous year. Glove You Little Sweetie and the Bedroom Tidies could still be found too, and several of the Heritage Bears remained, although the Traffic Warden and the Oxford Don had gone, and there was a new Soldier Bear in their place.

Other designs not among the previous year's toys included three huggable Beans 'n' Bears, measuring 9 to 14 inches (23 to 35.5cm) and four Oak Leaf Bears (16 to 26 inches, or 40.5 to 66cm), with an oak leaf on their left footpads. Versions of both had appeared in a 1999 supplement to the main catalogue, and could be found

The Oak Leaf Bears were first seen in 2001, in four sizes.

among the collectable bears in the 2000 catalogue. A smartly dressed, standing Millionaire Bear, measuring 36 inches (91.5cm), had appeared halfway through 2000, while the Rockers - something for which Merrythought has long been renowned - included a new and adorable Honey Bear alongside all the other animals.

It was still there in 2002. So were the panda and koala, the Bedroom Tidies, Glove You Little Sweetie and Topsy, although she was now available only in the 16 and 20 inch sizes (40.5 and 51cm) alongside the nightdress case version. The Toy Chest Bears were still there as well (although now described simply as Bear), as were all the Heritage Bears, the Bears 'n' Beans and the Oak Leaf Bears. There were no changes to the London Gold mohair bears, the Honey Growler Bears or any of the Ironbridge Bears either, but the Millionaire Bear had gone and there were several new, fully jointed bears.

Among them were the Curly Black and Curly Gold Pure Mohair Bears - both of which were offered in three sizes - 10, 14 and 18 inches (25.5, 35.5 and 45.5cm) - and there were also three sizes for the imposing William (namely 14, 18 and 21 inches, or 35.5, 45.5 and 53.5cm). His name appeared on his left footpad. Such designs helped to blur the distinction between the toys and the

collectables, which were once again included in a single catalogue. The collectables will be described in detail in the following chapter.

ABOVE: *The Millionaire Bear measured a sizable 36 inches (91.5cm) and was on sale for just one year (2001).*

LEFT: *The Soldier Bear (left) appeared in 2001, while the Household Cavalry Bear (centre) was first seen in 1996 and the Chef (right) a year later.*

Classic, jointed teddy bears

1990

GM London Gold Bear (mohair) in sizes 12, 14, 16, 18 (also with growl or music box), 21, 26, 32 and 40 inches (30.5, 35.5, 40.5, 45.5, 53.5, 66, 81.5 and 101.5cm)

MM London Gold Bear (synthetic plush) in sizes 10, 12, 14, 16, 18 (also with growl or music box), 21, 26, 32 and 40 inches (25.5, 30.5, 35.5, 40.5, 45.5, 53.5, 66, 81.5 and 101.5cm); also 14 inch (35.5cm) Bedtime Bear in nightshirt and cap

CM Butterscotch Bear (synthetic plush) in sizes 13, 17, 21 and 26 inches (33, 43, 53.5 and 66cm)

AR Nutmeg Bear (synthetic plush) in sizes 18, 22 and 26 inches (45.5, 56 and 66cm)

P Ironbridge Bear, measuring 10 inches (25.5cm), in Black, Fawn, and Silver-Grey synthetic plushes and London Gold mohair

TM5 London Gold Miniature Bear (mohair), 5 inches (12.5cm) – boxed

---

1991

GM London Gold Bear (mohair) in sizes 12, 14, 16, 18 (also with growl or music box), 21, 26, 32 and 40 inches (30.5, 35.5, 40.5, 45.5, 53.5, 66, 81.5 and 101.5cm)

MM London Gold Bear (synthetic plush) in sizes 10, 12, 14, 16, 18 (also with growl or music box), 21, 26, 32 and 40 inches (25.5, 30.5, 35.5, 40.5, 45.5, 53.5, 66, 81.5 and 101.5cm); also 14 inch (35.5cm) Bedtime Bear in nightshirt and cap

CM Butterscotch Bear (synthetic plush) in sizes 13, 17, 21 and 26 inches (33, 43, 53.5 and 66cm)

AR Nutmeg Bear (synthetic plush) in sizes 18, 22 and 26 inches (45.5, 56 and 66cm)

P Ironbridge Bear, measuring 10 inches (25.5cm), in Black, Fawn, and Silver-Grey synthetic plushes and London Gold mohair

[From 1991 onwards, the TM5 London Gold Miniature Bear (mohair) was included in the International Collectors' Catalogue]

1992

GM London Gold Bear (mohair) in sizes 12, 14, 16, 18 (also with growl or music box), 21, 26, 32 and 40 inches (30.5, 35.5, 40.5, 45.5, 53.5, 66, 81.5 and 101.5cm)

MM London Gold Bear (synthetic plush) in sizes 10, 12, 14, 16, 18 (also with growl or music box), 21, 26, 32 and 40 inches (25.5, 30.5, 35.5, 40.5, 45.5, 53.5, 66, 81.5 and 101.5cm); also 14 inch (35.5cm) Night Shirt Bear (as previous years' Bedtime Bear) in nightshirt and cap

AF Chocolate Bear (synthetic plush) in sizes 14, 17, 21 and 26 inches (35.5, 43, 53.5 and 66cm)

AR Nutmeg Bear (synthetic plush) in sizes 18, 22 and 26 inches (45.5, 56 and 66cm)

P Ironbridge Bear, measuring 10 inches (25.5cm), in Black, Fawn, and Silver-Grey synthetic plushes and London Gold mohair

---

1993

GM London Gold Bear (mohair) in sizes 12, 14, 16, 18 (also with growl or music box), 21, 26, 32 and 40 inches (30.5, 35.5, 40.5, 45.5, 53.5, 66, 81.5 and 101.5cm)

WG Classic Teddy Bear (synthetic plush) in sizes 10, 12, 14, 16, 18 (also with growl or music box), 21, 26, 32 and 40 inches (25.5, 30.5, 35.5, 40.5, 45.5, 53.5, 66, 81.5 and 101.5cm)

P Ironbridge Bear, measuring 10 inches (25.5cm), in Black, Fawn, Silver-Grey and Chocolate synthetic plushes and London Gold mohair

---

1994

GM London Gold Bear (mohair) in sizes 10, 12, 14, 16, 18 (also with growl or music box), 21, 26, 32 and 40 inches (25.5, 30.5, 35.5, 40.5, 45.5, 53.5, 66, 81.5 and 101.5cm)

FM Classic Teddy Bear (synthetic plush) in sizes 10, 12, 14, 16, 18 (also with growl or music box), 21, 26, 32 and 40 inches (25.5, 30.5, 35.5, 40.5, 45.5, 53.5, 66, 81.5 and 101.5cm)

P Ironbridge Bear, measuring 10 inches (25.5cm), in Black, Fawn, Silver-Grey and Chocolate synthetic plushes and London Gold mohair

James, made from pale gold mohair in 15 and 21 inch sizes (38 and 53.5cm)

1995

GM London Gold Bear (mohair) in sizes 10, 12, 14, 16, 18 (also with growl or music box), 21, 26, 32 and 40 inches (25.5, 30.5, 35.5, 40.5, 45.5, 53.5, 66, 81.5 and 101.5cm)

FM Classic Teddy Bear (synthetic plush) in sizes 10, 12, 14, 16, 18 (also with growl or music box), 21, 26, 32 and 40 inches (25.5, 30.5, 35.5, 40.5, 45.5, 53.5, 66, 81.5 and 101.5cm)

P Ironbridge Bear, measuring 10 inches (25.5cm), in Black, Fawn and Chocolate synthetic plushes and London Gold mohair

The Laird, made from mohair with plaid paw pads in 15 and 21 inch sizes (38 and 53.5cm)

1996

GM London Gold Bear (mohair) in sizes 10, 12, 14, 16, 18 (also with growl or music box), 21, 26, 32 and 40 inches (25.5, 30.5, 35.5, 40.5, 45.5, 53.5, 66, 81.5 and 101.5cm)

FM Classic Teddy Bear (synthetic plush) in sizes 10, 12, 14, 16, 18 (also with growl or music box), 21, 26, 32 and 40 inches (25.5, 30.5, 35.5, 40.5, 45.5, 53.5, 66, 81.5 and 101.5cm)

CM Champagne Bear (synthetic plush) in sizes 18, 21 and 26 inches (45.5, 53.5 and 66cm)

P Ironbridge Bear, measuring 10 inches (25.5cm), in Black and Chocolate synthetic plushes, and in Gold and Coffee mohairs

1997

GM London Gold Bear (mohair) in sizes 10, 12, 14, 16, 18 (also with growl or music box), 21, 26, 32 and 40 inches (25.5, 30.5, 35.5, 40.5, 45.5, 53.5, 66, 81.5 and 101.5cm)

JA Shropshire Pure Mohair Bear in sizes 10, 12, 14, 16 (also with growl or music box), 20 and 26 inches (25.5, 30.5, 35.5, 40.5, 51 and 66cm)

MJA Shropshire Classic Bear (synthetic plush) in sizes 14, 16 (also with growl or music box), 20 and 26 inches (35.5, 40.5, 51 and 66cm)

P Ironbridge Bear, measuring 10 inches (25.5cm), in Black and Chocolate synthetic plushes, and in Gold and Coffee mohairs

P Ironbridge Autumn Bears, made from a sparse mohair in sizes 8, 10, 13, 15, 17 and 20 inches (20.5, 25.5, 33, 38, 43 and 51cm)

1998

GM London Gold Bear (mohair) in sizes 10, 12, 14, 16, 18 (also with growl or music box), 21, 26, 32 and 40 inches (25.5, 30.5, 35.5, 40.5, 45.5, 53.5, 66, 81.5 and 101.5cm)

JA Shropshire Pure Mohair Bear in sizes 10, 12, 14, 16 (also with growl or music box), 20 and 26 inches (25.5, 30.5, 35.5, 40.5, 51 and 66cm)

HJA Shropshire Classic Bear (synthetic plush) in sizes 14, 16 (also with growl or music box), 20 and 26 inches (35.5, 40.5, 51 and 66cm)

P Ironbridge Bear, measuring 10 inches (25.5cm), in Black, Honey, Nutmeg, Caramel and Baroque Gold synthetic plushes, and in Gold mohair

P Ironbridge Barley Bear, made from mohair in sizes 8, 10, 13, 15, 17 and 20 inches (20.5, 25.5, 33, 38, 43 and 51cm)

Cookie, measuring 20 inches (51cm) and made from rust-coloured plush

1999

GM London Gold Bear (mohair) in sizes 10, 12, 14, 16, 18 (also with growl or music box), 21, 26, 32 and 40 inches (25.5, 30.5, 35.5, 40.5, 45.5, 53.5, 66, 81.5 and 101.5cm)

JA Shropshire Pure Mohair Bear in sizes 10, 12, 14, 16 (also with growl or music box), 20 and 26 inches (25.5, 30.5, 35.5, 40.5, 51 and 66cm)

P Ironbridge Bear, measuring 10 inches (25.5cm), in Black, Nutmeg, and Baroque Gold synthetic plushes, and in Gold and shaggy cream mohair

P Ironbridge Shortcake Bear, made from pale biscuit-coloured mohair in sizes 8, 10, 13, 15 (also with growl or music box), 17 and 20 inches (20.5, 25.5, 33, 38, 43 and 51cm)

Cookie, measuring 20 inches (51cm) and made from rust-coloured plush

Pewter, measuring 16 inches (40.5cm) and made from silver-grey plush

2000

GM London Gold Bear (mohair) in sizes 10, 12, 14, 16, 18 (also with growl or music box), 21, 26, 32 and 40 inches (25.5, 30.5, 35.5, 40.5, 45.5, 53.5, 66, 81.5 and 101.5cm)

MM Honey Growler Bear in sizes 12, 14, 16, 18, 21, 26, 32 and 40 inches (30.5, 35.5, 40.5, 45.5, 53.5, 66, 81 and 101.5cm)

P Ironbridge Bear, measuring 10 inches (25.5cm), in Black, Nutmeg, Silver and Sand Stone synthetic plushes, and in Gold and shaggy cream mohair

P Ironbridge Shortcake Bear, made from pale biscuit-coloured mohair in sizes 8, 10, 13, 15 (also with growl or music box), 17 and 20 inches (20.5, 25.5, 33, 38, 43 and 51cm)

Cookie, measuring 20 inches (51cm) and made from rust-coloured plush

Pewter, measuring 16 inches (40.5cm) and made from silver-grey plush

2001

GM London Gold Bear (mohair) in sizes 10, 12, 14, 16, 18 (also with growl or music box), 21, 26, 32 and 40 inches (25.5, 30.5, 35.5, 40.5, 45.5, 53.5, 66, 81.5 and 101.5cm)

MM Honey Growler Bear in sizes 12, 14, 16, 18, 21, 26, 32 and 40 inches (30.5, 35.5, 40.5, 45.5, 53.5, 66, 81 and 101.5cm)

P Ironbridge Bear, measuring 10 inches (25.5cm), in Black, Nutmeg, Silver and Sand Stone synthetic plushes, and in Gold and shaggy Cream mohair

P Ironbridge Shortcake Bear, made from pale biscuit-coloured mohair in sizes 8, 10, 13, 15 (also with growl or music box), 17 and 20 inches (20.5, 25.5, 33, 38, 43 and 51cm)

Oak Leaf Bears in sizes 16, 18, 21 and 26 inches (40.5, 45.5, 53.5 and 66cm)

2002

GM London Gold Bear (mohair) in sizes 10, 12, 14, 16, 18 (also with growl or music box), 21, 26, 32 and 40 inches (25.5, 30.5, 35.5, 40.5, 45.5, 53.5, 66, 81.5 and 101.5cm)

MM Honey Growler Bear in sizes 12, 14, 16, 18, 21, 26, 32 and 40 inches (30.5, 35.5, 40.5, 45.5, 53.5, 66, 81 and 101.5cm)

P Ironbridge Bear, measuring 10 inches (25.5cm), in Black, Nutmeg, Silver and Sand Stone synthetic plushes, and in Gold and shaggy Cream mohair

P Ironbridge Shortcake Bear, made from pale biscuit-coloured mohair in sizes 8, 10, 13, 15 (also with growl or music box), 17 and 20 inches (20.5, 25.5, 33, 38, 43 and 51cm)

Oak Leaf Bears in sizes 16, 18, 21 and 26 inches (40.5, 45.5, 53.5 and 66cm)

Curly Gold Pure Mohair Bear in sizes 10, 14 and 18 inches (25.5, 35.5 and 45.5cm)

Curly Black Pure Mohair Bear in sizes 10, 14 and 18 inches (25.5, 35.5 and 45.5cm)

William in sizes 14, 18 and 21 inches (35.5, 45.5 and 53.5cm)

Chapter 10

10. BEARS FOR COLLECTORS

1990–1

Although Merrythought produced a number of limited-edition bears for collectors during the 1980s, these were not available on a worldwide scale – but then, in 1990, the firm marked its 60th anniversary with a very special Diamond Jubilee Bear. Not only was he in a limited edition (of 2,500) to increase his appeal to collectors, but he was also available throughout the world.

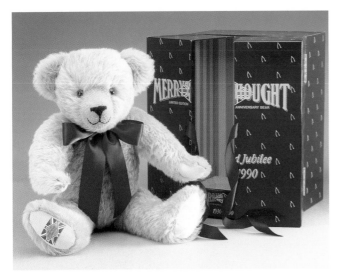

The boxed Jubilee Bear was made in 1990 to mark Merrythought's Diamond Jubilee.

Measuring 18 inches (45.5cm) in height, he was a classic, fully jointed ted, and was made from an exclusive "feather finish" mohair with sueded cotton pads. One of them carried a special woven label, with the Merrythought Jubilee logo superimposed on a Union Jack. The bear came in a special, hand-made, presentation box, with brass-hinged front "doors", and inside was a numbered certificate of authenticity, to coincide with the number on the limited-edition tag that was sewn into one of the side seams on the body.

He was launched at Harrods department store in London on Saturday 26 May, with Managing Director Oliver Holmes and Sales Director Jim Matthews both on hand to sign the pads of examples that were sold. But he was also soon on his way to other stores throughout Britain and the rest of the world, and quickly sold out.

He was the only limited edition in the 1990 catalogue, but by the end of the year a range of Euro

The Euro Bears, first seen in 1990, were among the first Merrythoughts to be made for collectors all over the world.

Bears had been introduced. Although they were unlimited, Merrythought made it clear that they had been produced with collectors in mind. There were four versions, each made in two sizes (14 and 18 inches/35.5 and 45.5cm), and all were both fully jointed and made from mohair.

A plain, toffee-coloured fabric was used for the London Euro Bear, while that representing Rome was in a spice brown. The Paris version, on the other hand, was in a brown-tipped blond fabric, while tipped apricot was used for that named after the German city of Bonn.

The city names were later dropped, but when Merrythought introduced its first special International Collectors' Catalogue in 1991, three of the four Euro Bears were included in it – that in toffee-coloured mohair and the two tipped versions. All three were unlimited.

A few of the other lines in the new Collectors' Catalogue were also unlimited but most were in small editions – some containing as few as 500. Almost all were also made from traditional mohair, to add to their appeal to serious enthusiasts, and they included many totally new designs as well as some variations on old favourites like the Cheeky. There were also versions of one or two earlier designs that had not previously been available to all collectors.

Star of the range was the brand-new Wellington. One of the totally original offerings, he was a very aristocratic ted in a vibrant gold mohair with a special swirled finish. One of his most distinctive features was his pronounced snout, on which the mohair had been shaved to show off his features to their best advantage. He was offered in two sizes – 15 inches and 21 inches (38 and 53.5cm) – with each limited to 2,500.

Isabel and Jeremy were designed by John Axe, author of The Magic of Merrythought.

Mohair with a special finish was used for Wellington, who was available in two sizes and launched the first International Collectors' Catalogue.

The two unlimited Cheeky Bears, on the other hand, were new variants on a bear first seen more than three decades before. Both were made from a relatively short-pile mohair – one in pale gold and one in a darker bronze – but the inset velveteen muzzles of the original Cheekys had given way to clipped mohair ones. Both bears were available in a single 12 inch (30.5cm) size.

Some of the other designs in the first International Collectors' Catalogue were variations on ones that had originally been on sale only in the United States. A larger version of Jeremy – designed by American John Axe, author of *The Magic of Merrythought* – had appeared in 1989, for example, and won a Golden Teddy Award from American magazine *Teddy Bear Review*. The new 14 inch (35.5cm) version wore a rosette commemorating this win. He was joined by a new John Axe design, the 15 inch (38cm) Isabel, made from gold mohair and wearing a red ribbon around her head. Both of these designs were in worldwide editions of 2,500.

The first Wiltshire Bear had been another US exclusive, inspired by an old ted given to Linda Smith of Tide-Rider, the distributors of Merrythought bears and toys in the United States. That bear's original owner lived in Wiltshire, England, and it was this that had given the bear his name. Two versions had appeared in the 1988 Tide-Rider catalogue, and two more were included in the first International Collectors' Catalogue. One was in a tipped mohair and one in a soft and silky pale gold. Both measured 15 inches (38cm) and were in limited editions of 500.

The first Elizabethan Bears had likewise been produced as exclusives for the American market (in 1986). Others had followed, and were again on sale only in the US, but there were three in the 1991 worldwide catalogue – 11 inch (28cm) examples in bright yellow or delicate pink mohair, and a 14 inch (35.5cm) gold one. All were limited to 500.

The white Miniature Bear had also been on sale in the USA for several years, but in 1991 it too became available worldwide, joining the gold one of the same size (5 inches/12.5cm) that had been a part of the regular Merrythought range. Both were unlimited, as was a new grey version that was seen for the first time in 1991.

Similarly, two of the 10 inch (25.5cm) pure mohair Ironbridge Bears (those in apricot and tipped apricot shades) were first seen in the USA – in 1989. But in 1991 they became available to all, along with a brand-new version in pure white mohair. All were limited to 1,000.

Another new arrival in 1991 was a gold version of the 17 inch (43cm) Magnet Bear – a replica of a 1930s design, in a limited edition of 1,000. A previous replica of this bear, in Honey mohair, had been launched by Tide-Rider in 1988 – as had two 6 inch (15cm) miniature Magnets in gold and tipped beige. But the 1991 replica was on worldwide sale, as were two new miniature Magnets, in Toffee and Bronze mohairs, which were both limited to 500.

The Toffee Nose Bear, on the other hand, first appeared in the United States in 1989 under the name Toffe Bear. He measured 12 inches (30.5cm) and was limited to 500. The 16 inch (40.5cm) Ascot Bears were the latest in the Edwardian Collection, and featured in the 1990 Tide-Rider Catalogue. Available in black or white mohair, and wearing contrasting striped bows, they were each in a limited edition of 1,000. All were now available in other countries.

Other bears in the 1991 International Collectors' Catalogue included the Rose Petal and Lavender Sachet Bears – each measuring 6 inches (15cm) and limited to 500. Both also appeared in the 1990 Tide-Rider Catalogue. There was a 21 inch (53.5cm), fully jointed, North American grizzly, as well – unlimited and and made from a luxurious synthetic plush. A traditional golly (unlimited) was introduced, as were two small mohair Bunnies – fully jointed and in editions of 500.

Bear-sized accessories in the 1991 International Collectors' Catalogue included a muff, backpack and finger puppet.

There were some bear-sized accessories too – namely a muff, backpack, glove puppet, shoulder bag and slippers. The Merrythought brooch and beaker – first seen in the 1989 soft toy catalogue – were also illustrated, and the 1991 collectors' range was completed by a replica of the 1932 Merrythought catalogue.

Master Mischief and Miss Mischief – both in limited editions of 1,500 – were popular new arrivals in 1992.

John Axe's Isabel and Jeremy appeared again in the 1992 International Collectors' Catalogue, as did both of the Wellingtons. But most of the pages were filled with brand-new designs by Merrythought's Design Director Jacqueline Revitt. Among them was one of her most successful designs ever – Master Mischief. He went on to win a TOBY Award from the American magazine *Teddy Bear and friends* – being the Public's Choice in the "Character Teddy, Manufactured" category – as well as a Golden Teddy Award from American magazine *Teddy Bear Review*.

The initial idea for the design had come to Jackie when she was watching her nephew being told off for some misdemeanour. She gave the bear a similar "butter wouldn't melt in his mouth" expression, but the paws clasped behind his back told a different story. Tightly held between them was a catapult. The catalogue picture carried the caption "I didn't break the window…"

There was a Miss Mischief as well, with red lips and cheeks and holding a little make-up bag in her paws.

This time the caption read "I haven't seen mummy's makeup..." Both bears were made in a short-pile mohair, with dungarees for him and a dress for her, and were complete with growls. They measured 16 inches (40.5cm) and were in boxed limited editions of 1,500.

An 18 inch (45.5cm), boxed Yes/No Bear was likewise limited to 1,500. Made from a blond mohair, with a black and white tie around his neck, he had a small tail which could be moved up and down or from side to side, causing him to nod or shake his head. The same edition

The 1992 Bingie Bear used a pattern that dated back to 1930; only the head and arms were jointed.

size was also chosen for the unboxed, 9 inch (23cm) Bingie Bear – a replica of the Bingie cub that appeared in the firm's first-ever catalogue. Made from mohair, it had jointed head and arms but was in a permanently seated position.

Merrythought opted for much larger editions, of 5,000, for two special commemorative bears, both of which were sold in specially decorated, hand-made boxes, with "doors" that could be opened to display the bears.

The Titanic Bear marked the 80th anniversary of the sinking of the RMS Titanic on 15 April 1912. He was based on a small bear that had been given to Catering Manager Gaspare Gatti by his son Vittorio when Gatti set sail on the ill-fated liner. Gatti was one of more than 1,500 who perished when the ship hit an iceberg. But the little bear apparently survived, and was eventually returned to his widow.

At 9 inches (23cm), Merrythought's version was slightly larger than the original, but it proved enormously popular with both bear lovers and collectors of Titanic memorabilia. By the time the next year's catalogue appeared, over 2,000 had already been sold; the remaining 500 disappeared soon afterwards.

The bear that Vittorio Gatti gave to his father was made long before Merrythought itself was founded. But the other commemorative bear to be launched in 1992 was a replica of a Merrythought design from the 1950s. At that time it was known as Woppit – a character that appeared in the children's weekly comic *Robin*. But one of the toys was given as a mascot to Donald Campbell, who broke many land and water speed records during the 1950s and 1960s (see also the chapter on the 1960s).

Campbell changed the name to Mr Whoppit, and the pair were inseparable, surviving several spectacular crashes before the one on Coniston Water in the Lake District, that took Campbell's life in 1967. Mr Whoppit was later found floating on the surface of the lake and duly rescued, although it would be more than 30 years before any trace of Campbell himself, and his boat *Bluebird*, was found. Merrythought used its original patterns to make the unjointed Mr Whoppit replica, with his blue feet and ear linings, and wearing a red jacket, just like the original.

Totally new designs for 1992, on the other hand, included the 18 inch (45.5cm) Stately Home Bear – made in a luxurious, dense mohair, and limited to 1,000. A

The 1992 Mr Whoppit was a replica of a bear that broke a string of land and water speed records with Donald Campbell.

String Mohair Bear (made from natural, loom-state mohair), and the Touch of Silk Bear, in a beautiful mohair and silk mix, were both of a similar size, and again in editions of 1,000. But many of the 1992 designs were even more limited, to just 500 in all.

Among these were the bent-legged Beanie Bear, in tipped mohair, and the Curly Bean Bear, in a synthetic plush reminiscent of Persian lamb. Both measured 16 inches (40.5cm) and, as their names suggest, were partly bean-filled to make them extra-posable.

The 1992 Attic Bear was made in a synthetic plush with a Persian lamb effect.

Curly Bean Bear and Beanie Bear were fully jointed, long-limbed teds with beans in their fillings to make them more posable.

Mohair Bride and Groom Bears, measuring 14 and 15 inches respectively (35.5 and 38cm) were in equally small editions – the bride accessorised with a veil and the groom with a collar and bow-tie. There were just 500 examples of the 9 inch (23cm) dressed bears Peter and Rosie too. Peter, made from gold mohair, wore a blue and white knitted play suit while the pure white Rosie, also mohair, was given a pretty white dress.

A new version of the Wiltshire Bear, again measuring 15 inches (38cm) but this time in peach-coloured mohair, was likewise limited to 500, and so was a beautiful new Tipped Cheeky in a silky long-pile mohair. Measuring 14 inches (35.5cm), he had a shaved muzzle instead of the more traditional velveteen but, like the classic Cheeky, was fully jointed with bells in his ears.

There were only 500 Mini Attic Bears as well – an 8 inch (20.5cm) mohair version of a design that had previously been on sale in the London department store Harrods. There was a "full-size" Attic Bear as well,

measuring 18 inches (45.5cm) and made from a "Persian lamb effect" synthetic cloth. That, however, was in a much larger and boxed edition of 1,500.

A new 10 inch (25.5cm) Ironbridge Bear, on the other hand – this time in buttermilk mohair – was limited to 1,000. So were two new mohair sachet bears, Peach Blossom and Spring Primrose, whose mohair and perfumes corresponded to their names. A 6 inch (15cm) Magnet Bear in black feathered mohair was also in an edition of that size, but some other collectors' designs were still unlimited.

They included a classic 10 inch (25.5cm) Cheeky, made from gold mohair with a velveteen muzzle, as well as the gold, white and grey miniatures that were to be found in the previous year's catalogue. A family of four was also unrestricted. Designed by illustrator and author Prue Theobalds, they all featured in her book *The Bears' Seaside Adventure*. Father Mortimer, measuring 18 inches (45.5cm) wore a smart waistcoat and bow-tie. Mother Martha (16 inches/40.5cm) was given a pretty floral apron. The 14 inch (35.5cm) Max was kept warm by a bright green sweater and checked scarf, while baby Marigold (8 inches/20.5cm) had a blue dress. All were fully jointed and made from mohair in traditionally bearish shades.

Mortimer, Martha, Max and Marigold were all designed by Prue Theobalds.

All the bear-sized accessories from the previous year, along with the bear-shaped brooch and the teddy-decorated beaker, were also still on sale, and the collectors' range was completed by the same handful of non-bear items.

The 1993 International Collectors' Catalogue contained an even wider range of totally new designs and variations on existing themes, together with a few bears from previous catalogues. Prue Theobalds' family of four were still there, for instance, as were the 9 inch (23cm) Bingie Bear and the boxed Mr Whoppit. The last 500 Titanic Bears were still included, and so were the two sizes of Wellington Bear, the Yes/No Bear, the Tipped Cheeky, the bear-sized accessories, the brooch and the beaker.

The London Gold Miniature Bear was retained as well – although he was now known as the London Gold Mini Bear – but the grey and white versions had disappeared. In their place were four new, palm-sized Mini Bears in pink, red, cream and brown-tipped mohair. Like their predecessors, all were fully jointed and measured just 5 inches (12.5cm) but, unlike the gold mini, they were all in limited editions of just 500 to increase their appeal to collectors.

Other new variations of earlier favourites included an 8 inch (20.5cm) Little Master Mischief, who was rightly

expected to be enormously popular and was therefore in a sizable edition of 2,000. Junior versions of the two John Axe bears – the same size as the new Master Mischief and going by the names of Jeremy Junior and Isabelita – were limited to 1,000 each, while the new Attic Bear, this time measuring just 6 inches (15cm), was restricted to just 500. So was the new Cheeky. Made from a bright yellow mohair with traditional velveteen muzzle and felt pads, he measured just 8 inches (20.5cm), and was known as the Squeaky Cheeky on account of the squeaker in his tummy.

The totally new designs for the year included a magnificent special-edition Rupert, dressed in the bear's familiar red sweater and yellow-checked trousers and scarf. Fully jointed and measuring 18 inches (45.5cm), he had mohair head and paws but, in the tradition of the

A special collectors' Rupert was produced for eight years during the 1990s.

1930s dressed Bingie Bears, the body and limbs under the clothes were made of a smoother cloth. Smart white shoes on his feet completed the look.

Although he was clearly aimed at collectors, he was not limited to a given number but to the time during which Merrythought retained the licence to produce him. In the event, he remained in production for eight years, and is now much-prized by enthusiasts. A 78-inch (nearly 2 metres) version was also available on special request.

Another character bear included in the 1993 International Collectors' Catalogue was Michael Bond's Paddington, but this was not actually the work of the Merrythought factory itself. It was the classic version of the famous bear, made in Yorkshire by Gabrielle Designs, and it was available for export only exclusively through Merrythought. It was just a brief experiment, however, and the bear had disappeared from the catalogue by the following year.

The Coronation Bear, first seen in 1993, was based on a design that first saw the light of day 40 years earlier.

Other designs new to the 1993 catalogue were all Merrythought's own work, and included two new commemoratives in hand-made boxes. The red, white and blue Coronation Bear was based on a Merrythought design from 1953. The new version, celebrating the 40th anniversary of the coronation of Queen Elizabeth II, was smaller, measuring just 8 inches (20.5cm).

The new Mount Everest Bear was the same size, and marked the 40th anniversary of the successful ascent of that mountain by Sir Edmund Hillary, who agreed to endorse the bear. Made in a glacier-grey mohair, the fully jointed ted came complete with his own ice pick and with a flag in his paw, ready for his own conquest of the mountain.

Both the new boxed bears were limited to 5,000, but the Connoisseur Teddy Bears, available in three sizes, were all unlimited. Made from brown mohair, with shaved muzzles, they were all fully jointed and measured

9, 14 and 26 inches (23, 35.5 and 66cm). A miniature Connoisseur Bear was available free to the buyer of one in every 100 of the larger bears.

Distinctive fabric or accessories were the striking features of a number of other new arrivals. The 9 inch (23cm) Mr Tweedle, for example, was created from a curled alpaca, and was made extra-posable by the beans in his tummy. Virgin wool was used for the 28 inch (71cm) Bear With No Name (intended as the perfect christening present). Reversed virgin wool provided an unusual finish for the aptly named Inside Out Bear, measuring 15 inches (38cm), and loom-state (or string) mohair was used for the little 7 inch (18cm) Kendal. All were in editions of just 500, with the exception of the Inside Out Bear, which was limited to 1,000.

String mohair was used again for the 16 inch (40.5cm) String Bean, which wore a striking ribbon in a colourful vegetable print. Like Bon Bon the Chocoholic – in the same size, and with a chocolate print ribbon – he was fully jointed with a bean-filled tummy, and was made in a limited edition of 1,000.

Colourful prints were used for the pads of four seasonal bears, and also for the collar, ruff or cravat around their necks. Spring was represented by Tulip Time, with mohair in a delicate shade of pink. Strawberry

The 1993 Ballerina was complete with tutu and ballet slippers.

Fayre was cream-coloured – a fitting accompaniment to the summery fruit on the collar and paws. Fruit Cup was in an autumnal brown, while winter's Snow Berry was pure white. All were fully jointed, measuring 10 or 11 inches (25.5 or 28cm), and limited to just 500.

Totally different again was the pale pink Ballerina, dressed in a net tutu and pink ballet slippers. Measuring 17 inches (43cm), she was in an edition of 1,000. So were two other 1993 dressed bears. The 15 inch (38cm) Grandma's Bear wore a lace-trimmed, white nightdress, while The Artist was given a white smock and black beret, as well as his own small palette and brush.

Movement was a feature of several 1993 designs, including the Attic Bear on a Trike and the Dancing Bear.

Special accessories also added extra interest to some other new designs. The 12 inch (30.5cm) Lost Property Bear – limited to 1,000 – was a classic, fully jointed, teddy in gold mohair, for instance, but a striking feature was that he came surrounded by tissue in his own brown-paper, lost-property bag. The Attic Bear on a Trike, on the other hand, was a 16 inch (40.5cm) version of an existing Merrythought favourite, but only his head was jointed. His legs were in the form of bright red trousers – specially hinged and attached to the pedals of his wooden tricycle, so that he appeared to be pedalling furiously when it was pulled along. He was limited to just 500.

Other forms of movement were also incorporated into some new bears. The 12 inch (30.5cm) Dancing Bear twirled round on his wooden base while his music box

A unique mechanism was incorporated into the 1993 Clapping Bear.

was playing, and the Hold Me Tight or Clapping Bear clapped his hands when his body was squeezed. The Dancing Bears were limited to just 500; the Clapping Bears were in an edition of 1,500.

Totally different again was the 12 inch (30.5cm) Teddy Do Fings, that was based on a 1930s design. A specially articulated body meant that his arms and legs could be placed in countless different positions, enabling him to sit, stand, wave his paws and more. Made from traditional mohair, he was limited to just 500.

The only other bear in the catalogue was the 16 inch (40.5cm) T.J. Bear. Made from a classic, short-pile gold mohair with black felt pads and a black and silver bow, he was fully jointed and in an edition of 1,000. In addition, there were again two gollies (one new), as well as three replicas of 1930s felt dolls to complete the 1993 range.

One of the dolls, Emily, returned the following year, along with a new Manageress doll, carrying a small teddy in one hand and her design notes in the other. But

(Left to right) Grandma's Bear and the Artist were first seen in 1993, but Rusty and the Little Drummer Boy were new in 1994.

although there were again two gollies (one of them new), and a delightful version of G.E. Studdy's dog Bonzo, the 1994 International Collectors' Catalogue was once more largely filled with bears. The only other exception was a 9 inch (23cm) version of Rupert's friend Bill Badger, which was introduced in an edition of 10,000 along with a similarly sized Rupert that was to be limited to the same number.

The larger Rupert, first seen the previous year, was still there as well, while other familiar faces were the three Connoisseur Bears, the London Gold Mini Bear, the Artist, Grandma's Bear, the two small versions of the John Axe bears, the Prue Theobalds family and the boxed Mr Whoppit, Coronation Bear and Mount Everest Bear. Still on offer, too, were the bear-sized accessories, the beaker and the brooch, but a short-sleeved green polo shirt, a watch (featuring four teddies on its face) and a miniature passport were among the new items, that naturally also included a good number of bears.

Again, the designs covered a wide range, with interesting fabrics, clothing, accessories and ingenious mechanisms helping to add extra interest. There were new musical bears, for example - this time all of them dressed. The Ice Skater, in her blue and white cloak and white lace-up boots, glided round her turntable to the sound of a Strauss Waltz. Measuring 11 inches (28cm), she was limited to 1,000, as was the pirouetting Sugar Plum Fairy - 12 inches (30.5cm) in height.

There was a pair of Ballroom Dancers as well - she a picture in blue net and he wearing a smart black tail coat. Both bears were made from mohair (white and grey, respectively), and stood cheek to cheek on their own dance floor. The set had an overall height of 10 inches (25.5cm), and was limited to just 500.

There was a musical theme to the Little Drummer Boy as well - a 12 inch (30.5cm) bear, with a braid-trimmed hat and his own, bear-sized drum. A 13 inch (33cm) Marionette Bear, on the other hand, could be made to dance and perform various other antics, and was in a larger edition of 1,000.

In other cases, the most striking feature was the fabric. That used for Barton, for example, was specially from a beige-coloured distressed cotton. A smaller (15 inch/38cm) version of the Yes/No Bear was in an edition of 1,000, however, but no edition size was given for the six Micro Attic Bears. Measuring 6 inches (15cm), they included five in mohair – Light Gold, Black, Brandy, Peach and Tipped – while the sixth was made from distressed cotton.

A striking white collar as well as a blue bow was used as the finishing touch for the 10 inch (25.5cm) Baby Blue Eyes, again limited to just 500, but even more dramatic was the giant hat sported by the Hat Box Bear – made from a rich, claret-coloured brocade that was also used for the bear's pads. The 9 inch (23cm) bear was limited to 1,000 and came in a smart, hexagonal hat box in the same shade as the hat.

There were several fully dressed bears, too, with the 10 inch (25.5cm) Good Queen Bess the most elaborate – dressed in fine brocade, trimmed with gold, and limited to 500. Slightly smaller, at 9 inches (23cm) was The Auctioneer – wearing an 18th century style of costume, and complete with a hand-turned gavel in his paw. He, too, was limited to 500, as was the similarly sized Peek-a-Boo in his bright pink bunny suit. An edition size of 1,000 was chosen for the 14 inch (35.5cm) Cuthbert, however. He was described as everybody's favourite Grandpa, and was dressed in a green-spotted waistcoat made from the same velvet as his pads.

The Marionette Bear was one of the new designs in 1994.

developed to give him a "loved to pieces" look. Measuring 13 inches (33cm), he was another bear that was limited to just 500. So, too, was the colourful, 10 inch (25.5cm) Cotton Cutie – made from a cotton print fabric featuring antique toys, and with a squeaker inside his body. The smaller Cashmere – 9 inches (23cm) – was in a larger edition of 1,000, however. As his name suggests, he was made from pure cashmere, while pure silk was used for his pads and bow.

A bow was also the only accessory on the 15 inch (38cm) Anniversary Bear. In this case, though, the words Happy Anniversary were printed in gold on the ribbon. The bear itself was made from a sparse gold mohair, and was another design that was limited to just 500.

Other undressed bears among the newcomers for 1994 included the 20 inch (51cm) Rusty, with blond tips to much of his chocolate-brown mohair. He, too, was limited to 500, as was the 18 inch (45.5cm) Coco, made

Purest cashmere was used for Cashmere the bear – one of the favourites from the 1994 range.

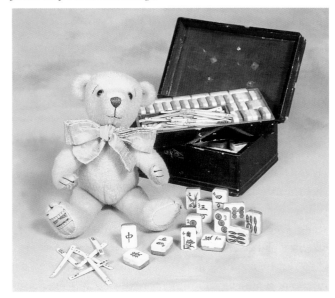

Also dressed were the four Nursery Rhyme characters, each measuring 12 inches (30.5cm) and in editions of 500. Tommy Tucker wore a blue and white striped playsuit, and a bib carrying the letter T. Mary Mary was given a crisp white pinafore over her frock. Twinkle Twinkle wore a white nightshirt trimmed with a starry print fabric that was also used for the cap, while Ride a Cock Horse wore a pretty print dress and carried her own wooden hobby horse.

Of all the new arrivals for 1994, however, it was perhaps the Micro Cheekys that caused the greatest stir. There were six of them in all – in Beige, Gold, Banana, Blue, Pink and Distressed mohairs – each measuring just 6 inches (15cm) and with the classic Cheeky grins embroidered over their inset muzzles. With edition sizes of just 500, it soon became obvious that there were far too few of them to satisfy the enormous demand, and by the summer a further three versions had been introduced. They were included in a supplement to the main catalogue. One was in a brilliant shade of red, another in a striking apricot mohair, tipped with brown, while the third was in a classic bronze shade. Again, each was limited to just 500.

The supplement also included new versions of other favourites from the main catalogue. The 9 inch (23cm) Cashmere bear had, as expected, captured many hearts, so a new 8 inch (20.5cm) Cashmere Cutie was introduced, again in an edition of 1,000. There was also a younger brother for the "loved to pieces" Barton – this time known as Barton Junior. Measuring 11 inches (28cm), he was fitted with a squeaker, and was again limited to just 500. The new Anniversary Bear, on the other hand, was in the same size as his predecessor, but in a blond distressed fabric instead of the previous gold. Once more, the edition size was just 500.

Clearly, even these new additions were not enough to satisfy many collectors, and when the 1995 catalogue appeared there were more Micro Cheekys, as well as another version of the Cashmere ted – this time known as the Cutie Cashmere and measuring a mere 6 inches (15cm). Again, he was fully jointed, limited to just 500, and made from pure cashmere with silk pads, but the large silk bow had given way to a more conventional blue one.

Bows were also the only adornment on four of the new Micro Cheekys – known as Old Gold, White, Grey and Spikey (the latter in a striking tipped fabric). But there were two ingenious new Micro Cheeky designs as well, and they helped to set a trend for the years that followed.

Cheeky on Parade was in the form of a Guardsman bear, with conventional blond mohair used for his head and feet, but with his body and arms bright red, to represent his jacket, and his legs black, to give the impression of trousers. On his head was a black busby – made, like the rest of the bear, from mohair.

Even more colourful was Cheeky Clowns Around, with his head, half his body, one arm and one leg in bright red mohair and the rest in bright blue. On his head was a red and white clown's hat, made from felt, and round his neck a felt ruff with red, white and blue layers. Like all the other new Micro Cheekys, he was fully jointed and limited to 500.

There were other new Cheekys as well. One was a bright-gold Yes/No bear, whose head could be made to move by twisting his tail. Measuring 12 inches (30.5cm), he wore a collar and tie, and was in an edition of 500. An even smaller edition, of just 250, was chosen for the Carousel that featured three golden yellow Micro Cheekys, seated on the swings of a wooden carousel that played music while it turned. There were also just 250 of the 26 inch (66cm) Corn Silk Cheeky – the largest of three classic mohair Cheekys. His smaller brothers measured 17 inches (43cm) and 15 inches (38cm) and were in editions of 500 and 1,000 respectively.

There were three new Micro Attic Bears as well – this time in Red, Ice White and Distressed mohair, and again limited to 1,000. A new version of the ever-popular Ironbridge Bear measured 10 inches (25.5cm) and was this time made from Sunset Gold mohair, in a limited edition of 500. Another variation on an existing bear was a Cutie Mohair brother for the Cutie Cashmere – made from a luxurious brown mohair in the same 6 inch (15cm) size, and limited to just 500.

The 1995 catalogue also included some designs that were unchanged from the previous year, however. The Hat Box Bear was still there, for example, as were the three Connoisseur Bears. So were the Little Drummer Boy and the musical Sugar Plum Fairy. The Manageress, with her little mohair teddy, was back as well – although this time there were no design notes in her paw – and other familiar faces included Rusty, Baby Blue Eyes, the Small Yes-No bear, the London Gold Mini, Cuthbert, the boxed Mr Whoppit, Rupert (both sizes) and his friend Bill Badger.

Good Queen Bess was back as well, and this time she was joined by the 11 inch (28cm) Henry VIII, in suitably regal attire and limited to 500. Jeremy Junior returned, but Isabelita's place at his side had been taken by a new John Axe design by the name of Goldie – a slim, 14 inch (35.5cm) mohair bear in an edition of 1,000. A new golly also joined the unlimited Velvet Golly that had been in the catalogue since 1991, and there were some changes to the bear-related items as well.

The Teddy Puppet and Teddy Slippers had disappeared, although the Pocket Book, Muff and Back Pack were still there. So were the brooch, the China Beaker, the Polo Shirt and the Miniature Replica Passport, and they had been joined by a number of new bear-related items. There was a white duffel bag, decorated with teddies, for example, while three other new pieces featured the popular Cheeky. Two of them – a pin and a charm – were in solid, hallmarked, English silver, while the third was a watch with four Cheekys pictured on its face.

Of course, there were also many totally new bears, in a wide range of designs and fabrics, and with most limited to no more than 1,000 – the exception being the Blue Sapphire Anniversary Bear that celebrated 65 years of Merrythought. Made from a striking blue mohair and sold in a special presentation case, this 7 inch (18cm) fully jointed design was limited to 2,500.

Totally different were the ponderous Blunder (16 inches/40.5cm) and the 9 inch (23cm) Bodger in their unusual curly mohair. Another curly mohair, this time in a typically bearish shade, was used for the saggy Rag Bag Bear – a totally relaxed and highly posable ted. Measuring 14 inches (35.5cm), he was in an edition of 500, as was the totally different paperboy ted, Read All About It. Made from a shaggy mohair, and fully jointed, he wore a cloth cap and carried a bag of Ironbridge Gazette 'newspapers'.

Streetwise "George" also wore a cap – in his case a baseball one, while on his feet were chunky shoes and socks. But this "bear with attitude" was said to be a softie at heart, in spite of his attempts at a mean expression.

Bodger (left) and Blunder were first seen in 1995, but returned again the following year.

Made from a shaggy mohair, and measuring 11 inches (28cm), he was limited to 500, as was the slightly larger City Slicker (12 inches/30.5cm), whose gold mohair had a shorter, straighter pile. A pin-striped waistcoat ensured that he was all ready for a trip to town.

Several other new dressed bears were also included in the 1995 catalogue. A Bingie Sea Captain was inspired by the dressed Bingie Bears of the 1930s. Wearing a white jacket and trousers, and a smart peaked cap, he had a mohair head, paws and feet, as did the Bingie Brigadier, who again was given a suitably smart uniform. Both measured 16 inches (40.5cm) and were in editions of 500, while a smaller Home Guard (12 inches/30.5cm), with only head and paws in mohair, was limited to 1,000.

Very different was Pippin, the Moulded Face Bear – a totally new design, made from tipped mohair and with a face created using an old mask. Measuring 11 inches (28cm), the unusual smiling ted was limited to 1,000.

So, too, were the 9 inch (23cm) Little Poppet – a fully jointed bear with a large organza bow – and the 11 inch (28cm) Appearance Bear, which was to be on sale only when Merrythought's Managing Director Oliver Holmes or Design Director Jacqueline Revitt were visiting a retailer to personally sign each of these special bears. An Imperial Bear in a rich, claret-coloured mohair with gold pads was likewise in an edition of 1,000, and so was the

(Left to right) Paleface, Streetwise "George", Read All About It and City Slicker were all new in 1995, while Cuthbert was first seen a year earlier.

fund-raising Great Ormond Street Children's Hospital Bear, that held a small blue blanket carrying the hospital's motif. For each example sold, Merrythought sent a donation of £5 to the hospital.

The remaining new designs for 1995 were all limited to just 500. They included two small (5 inch/12.5cm) Perfume Bottle Bears, in white or pink mohair, whose heads could be removed to reveal the bottle inside. Slightly larger, at 7 inches (18cm), was sweet-faced Lavender Blue, who took his name from the colour of his mohair, while at the other end of the scale was the giant 26 inch (66cm) Brindley, in a luxurious tipped fabric.

Also new were the 13 inch (33cm) Paleface, with his paler muzzle and tum contrasting with the golden brown used to make the rest of his head and body, and with contoured arms and legs. Then there was Allsorts, measuring 10 inches (25.5cm) and made from several different cotton print fabrics. The most striking feature of the 15 inch (38cm) Floppy Joe, on the other hand, was his extra-long limbs, while in the case of the 13 inch

(33cm) Amethyst, it was the rich colour of the fabric that made the greatest impression.

Very different again was the 13 inch (33cm) Baby's First Bear - made from mohair but in a soft and cuddly design. And the 1995 range was completed by the 11 inch (28cm) Special Occasion Bear - contained in a smart presentation box to make him an ideal gift for a special person or a special occasion.

No fewer than three of the 1995 designs - namely Floppy Joe, Paleface and Cheeky on Parade - brought Merrythought nominations for prestigious TOBY® Awards from the American magazine *Teddy Bear and friends*. But other editions also proved exceptionally popular, and again a special Summer Collection was launched to help fill some of the gaps left by editions that had sold out.

Again, the Cheekys has been especially in demand, and the new lines included two more Micro Cheekys, in Blush and Buttercup mohairs, with each limited to 500. There were three slightly larger Mini Cheekys, measuring 7 inches (18cm), as well - in Banana, Tipped and

New designs for 1995 included six Micro Cheekys and the moulded-face bear Pippin.

Distressed mohairs, respectively, and with each limited to 1,000. And a new Yes/No Golden Cheeky was made from a bright gold mohair with a pure white collar and a cheerful red and white cravat. Measuring 12 inches (30.5cm), he was again limited to just 500.

There was a brother for Floppy Joe as well – namely Floppy Jim, again measuring 15 inches (38cm) and limited to 500, but this time in a shaggier mohair. A new 6 inch (15cm) Caramel Cashmere had also been added to the cashmere range, in an edition of 500. Similarly limited were the other two new arrivals – the curly-haired Little Mo measuring 11 inches (28cm), and the 10 inch (25.5cm) Mummy Lavender, to go with the endearing Lavender Blue.

Paleface went on to win one of the coveted TOBY® Awards, and the 1996 catalogue celebrated the event by offering a smaller version – the 10 inch (25.5cm) Son of Paleface – alongside the original. Again he was limited to just 500. There was also a second brother for TOBY® nominee Floppy Joe – in the form of Floppy Ted, again measuring 13 inches (33cm) and limited to 500, but this time made from a relatively short-pile mohair.

There was a sister for the 1993 Little Master Mischief as well. Like him she was a miniature version of a 1992 design, measuring 8 inches (20.5cm) and in a relatively

large limited edition of 2,000. The new Yes-No Mischief, on the other hand, was limited to just 500. Measuring 16 inches (40.5cm), and accessorized only with a red scarf, he could be made to nod or shake his head by twisting his tail.

A new mohair Ironbridge Bear, measuring 10 inches (25.5cm), was introduced as well, in an edition of 500. And there were also several new versions of the ever-popular Cheeky, including another six of the 6 inch (15cm) Micros, all of which were again limited to 500. Cheeky Lavender and Cheeky Amethyst were named after the colours of the fabric used to make them, while Cheeky on the Beat was a Micro policeman, complete with helmet. Cheekys Down the Aisle were a wedding couple – the bride complete with veil and bouquet and the groom sporting a top hat and bow tie – and the final bear in the series was Cheer Up Cheeky. He had special, soulful eyes with a glum, turned-down mouth instead of the usual Cheeky grin, and he carried a small handkerchief to dry his tears.

A more traditional version was the 12 inch (30.5cm) Musical Cheeky, wound up by a key in his back. Made from mohair with a fairly short pile, he wore a bow printed with the words "I play a tune" and was in an edition of just 500. So, too, were the new Mr and Mrs

Twisty Cheeky that re-created a 1960s design. Each measured 12 inches (30.5cm).

Following on from the success of the previous year's Corn Silk Cheeky, there was a new Cloud Silk version in the same three sizes, as well as a delightfully posable Cheeky Full of Beans, again in the three sizes. In each case, the 15 inch (38cm) size was once more limited to 1,000, while the 17 inch (43cm) bear was in an edition of 500, and there were just 250 of the largest (26 inch/66cm) versions.

The Carousel Cheekys from the previous year's catalogue reappeared in 1996, as did a number of other designs, including such enduring favourites as the London Gold Miniature, the two versions of Rupert, and his friend Bill Badger. The three Connoisseur Bears returned as well, as did the John Axe designs Jeremy Junior and Goldie, and the boxed replica of Mr Whoppit. Bodger, Blunder, Pippin, Streetwise "George", Little Poppet, Amethyst and the Imperial Bear were also familiar faces, as were Baby's First Bear, the Special Occasion Bear, the Home Guard, and the Great Ormond Street Children's Hospital Bear. But there were two new gollies as well as a whole host of brand-new bears, and a 12-inch (30.5cm) bear and golly set known as Play Mates, in an edition of 500.

An especially striking addition to the 1996 catalogue was a group of replicas of Alpha Farnell bears, which Merrythought had faithfully reproduced from the originals. They included a beautiful Alpha Bear, just like those that were on sale in the 1930s. Measuring a hefty 26 inches (66cm), he was a classic, fully jointed ted, with long arms and large feet, made from high-quality mohair and in an edition of just 500.

The other two Farnell designs were similarly limited. The Golden Mohair Bear was a 14 inch (35.5cm) charmer, with the shorter limbs and smaller feet of Farnell's later bears, while the 9 inch (23cm) Musical Bear was of a type first seen in 1937, and wore a fetching pink jacket.

There were replicas of early Merrythought designs as well. "Hans" Dutch Bear, for example, was based on a design first seen in the 1930s. This new version, measuring 15 inches (38cm), had head, body and arms made from gold mohair, while his legs were in the form of wide, Dutch-style trousers, made from a fitting windmill-print fabric.

A colourful print fabric was also used in the Print Teddy Replica, which re-created a 1940s design, produced at a time when mohair was in short supply. Like his predecessors, the new, unjointed, collectors' bear had only his head made from mohair, while his body and limbs were made from the printed cloth. He measured 13 inches (33cm) and, like the Dutch Bear, was in an edition of 500.

The little Toby Replica, made from a 1933 pattern, was similarly limited, and again had only his head made from mohair. Half his body as well as one leg and one arm were made from bright red cloth, while the remainder was dark blue, and round his neck was a yellow ruff. He measured just 8 inches (20.5cm).

Other designs were totally new, and included several that made use of bent arms or legs to add extra interest. Among them were the dapper Archie Major and Archie Junior, in their collars and ties – the larger measuring 23 inches (58.5cm) and the smaller 11 inches (28cm). Both were limited to 500, as was Uncle Walter, whose beard-like extra-long mohair around a partly shaved muzzle turned him into the old man of the collection. Measuring 20 inches (51cm), he had distinctive long, bent arms, curving down at the paws, which were complete with thumbs.

A beard turned Uncle Walter into the old man of the 1996 range.

God Bless Mummy, on the other hand, was a very young-looking bear, with long legs bent into a kneeling position, eyes firmly closed, and paws joined together in prayer under his chin. He measured just 8 inches (20.5cm) and, like many of that year's designs, was in an edition of 500.

There was an even younger look for the 9 inch (23cm) Little Sleepy Head, again limited to 500. Made from a classic gold mohair, with a lighter coloured body, he had his paws raised to rub the sleep from his eyes, and his own blue comfort blanket.

Other bears were more conventional. The 14 inch (35.5cm) Hawthorn, for example, was a classic, fully jointed, brown ted in an edition of 250 – the creation of a guest designer Joan Links. The two Pure Elegance bears (14 and 18 inches/35.5 and 45.5cm) were even more traditional. Made from blond mohair, they were reminiscent of examples from a bygone age, although both were totally new and limited to 500 each.

Quite different again was the 9 inch (23cm) Golden Dream, with his shiny gold pads and collar. He, too, was in an edition of 500, as was the 18 inch (45.5cm) musical Rainbow Bear.

Just a fraction of his size were the 8 inch (20.5cm) Choc-Ice and Biscuit, designed to be small enough to carry anywhere. A tipped chocolate mohair was used for Choc-Ice, whose muzzle was trimmed to reveal the rich brown underlying colour, while Biscuit's tightly curled fabric was, as the name suggests, Cookie-coloured. Both were limited to 500, as was the luxurious little velvet bear, known as Velveteenie and measuring 10 inches (25.5cm) from top to toe.

Like Choc-Ice and Biscuit, Velveteenie was accessorized with just a smart bow, but there were a few new dressed bears as well. Billy the Baker's Boy was designed to be reminiscent of 1930, in his cap and apron. He was 12 inches (30.5cm) in height, and restricted to 500, as were the 10 inch (25.5cm) Jack and Jill – made in toning shades of mohair with a dress for Jill and playsuit for Jack, and with a pail to carry the water.

The final new bear for the year was a 12 inch (30.5cm) Roller Bear on all fours, standing on a pull-along wooden trolley. This mohair bear was once more limited to 500.

So were three brand-new bearish accessories that appeared in the same catalogue. They included the Cheekies Cheek to Cheek nightdress case, which was based on earlier Merrythought designs that featured a velveteen bed with the heads of popular characters peering from them. This time the heads were of Cheeky bears – made from gold mohair with traditional velveteen muzzles and the familiar broad grin.

The Cheekies Cheek to Cheek nightdress case was based on Merrythought designs from the 1960s.

Muffs had also been made by Merrythought in various designs in the past, and 1996 saw a totally new one, based on the award-winning Paleface. The muff formed the bear's body, while attached to it were Paleface's distinctive head, with its contrasting muzzle, and his golden brown arms and legs. There was a new 25 inch (63.5cm) Back Pack Bear too – intended to be the perfect companion for fairs and conventions.

The bear-sized backpack remained as well, along with the miniature muff and pocket book, and so did the brooch, beaker, passport, Cheeky Pin and Cheeky Charm, although the watches had disappeared.

The bear-sized accessories, teddy brooch, silver Cheeky pin and charm, the china beaker and the miniature passport were again featured in the 1997 catalogue, but the limited-edition, human-sized accessories were no longer available, and only a handful of the other bears on offer that year had already appeared in previous catalogues. The two Ruperts and Bill Badger were still in the range, as were the London Gold Miniature Bear, the Great Ormond Street Bear and the boxed Mr Whoppit, but everything else was new – although they included some replicas of early designs and some new versions of popular collectors' bears.

The replicas included another Alpha Farnell design, this time made from a blond mohair and available in three sizes – 16, 20 and 26 inches (40.5, 51 and 66cm) – with editions of 1,000, 500 and 250 respectively. But many enthusiasts were delighted to see that there was a

A replica of an Alpha Farnell, in three sizes, was one of the new offerings in 1997.

reproduction of Merrythought's own Bobby Bruin as well. The original was launched in 1935, and was designed to be more like a real bear than a teddy. The new edition faithfully captured his look, but was available only in one size (14 inches/35.5cm), rather than the three that were made earlier. He was limited to just 750.

Another replica was of a rare red bear that had been acquired at auction by Merrythought. The old bear, dating from around the 1930s, had been left sitting in the sun, which had bleached his mohair, so the mohair for the new Sun Bleached bear was specially commissioned to reproduce that effect. The classic, fully jointed, 14 inch (35.5cm) bear featured the distinctive webbed claw stitching seen on many early Merrythoughts, and was limited to 750.

A bear called Colin was also a replica – of a ted that was featured in Pauline Cockrill's best-selling *Ultimate Teddy Bear Book*. At 14 inches (35.5cm) he was smaller than the original, and his gold mohair was also far less worn, but he had the distinctive look of the 1930s Magnet Bears as they were when still new. He was limited to just 1,000.

Velveteenie Junior was also based on a previous Merrythought bear, but in this case his predecessor dated from just one year earlier, when Velveteenie was launched. The new version was smaller, at 8 inches (20.5cm), but was again limited to 500. He was pictured with Ironbridge Frostie, made from a striking frosted

mohair, who again measured 8 inches (20.5cm), and was in another edition of 500.

There was another Mischief as well, this time a Micro version in his checked dungarees, and still complete with a tiny catapult behind his back. Measuring just 7 inches (18cm), he was again limited to 1,000 and became an instant favourite. There was a Micro version of God Bless Mummy too – once more kneeling with his paws together and his eyes tightly shut. Like the Micro Mischief, he measured just 7 inches (18cm), but the edition size was smaller, at 500.

There were new Micro Cheekys as well – this time a total of eight in all, each measuring 6 inches (15cm) and each again limited to 500. Three were classic in style, adorned only with a bow and taking their names – Starlight, Autumn and Pearl – from the colours of their mohair. But a combination of sewn-in and added clothing and accessories were used in the creation of the remaining five characters.

The bright-red Little Devil was given horns and a tail, while Oh La La wore a lace-trimmed white apron over her sewn-in black dress, and a lacy cap on her head. The Highlander was given a tartan kilt and tam-o'shanter, as well as a sewn-in red shirt. A colourful tunic and ribbon-trimmed hat made up the Beefeater's uniform, while the Father Christmas was given a traditional red coat and black trousers (both sewn-in), along with a fur-trimmed red hat.

There were larger Cheekys as well, including two sets of three that were in the same range of sizes as in the previous two years. Cheeky Azure was in a vibrant shade of blue, with a white muzzle and blue pads, while Fire Silk Cheeky was in a striking red mohair tipped with black, and was given coordinating black muzzle and black pads. As before, the 15 inch (38cm) size was limited to 1,000, while there were just 500 of the 17 inch (43cm) version, and only 250 of the largest (26 inch/66cm) size.

Coordinating colours were a feature of the Cheeky & Golly Set as well – measuring 8 inches (20.5cm) in height, and limited to 500 sets. Black mohair was used for the Cheeky, which had a golden yellow bow that matched the golly's bow tie. The golly's yellow jacket matched the bear's pads, while a black and white checked fabric was used for his trousers.

There were eight other gollies in the catalogue that year, including some novel new designs as well as one replica, and the new bears were equally innovative, although there were some classic examples as well.

Star of the year was Bearheart, more a real bear than a teddy, and designed to be as comfortable standing on his hind legs as sitting on his haunches. Fully jointed, he was made in two sizes, with the 14 inch (35.5cm) version limited to 750. His giant brother (measuring twice that size) was in an edition of only 50.

The 1997 Bearheart was more like a real bear than a teddy.

Only slightly smaller in height was the lanky Georgie Girl – a long-legged tomboy with distinctive upturned paws. Measuring 26 inches (66cm), she wore striped dungarees, and was limited to 250.

Equally distinctive in his own way was the rather bewildered-looking Stowaway, who came with his own wooden box to hide in. Measuring 10 inches (25.5cm), he was in an edition of 750. Then there was the 15 inch (38cm) Baby Baggy Bear that was destined to appear in a number of forms over the next few years. Fully jointed, he had a bean-filled tummy that made him especially

The tomboy Georgie Girl measured a sizable 26 inches (66cm), and was one of the new bears for 1997.

Various versions of the Baby Baggy Bear were produced; this one was in the 1997 catalogue.

pleasing to hold, as well as exceedingly posable. The version in the 1997 catalogue was limited to 750.

New dressed bears, on the other hand, included the 12 inch (30.5cm) Muffin Man, limited to 750, but a far smaller edition of just 250 was chosen for the 9 inch (23cm) William Schoolboy, in his school uniform. He was designed by the nine-year-old Beth Richards – winner of a junior design competition featured in the Merrythought International Collectors' Club Magazine.

Totally different again were the romantic Love in a Mist pair of 10 inch (25.5cm) bears, with their arms clasped tightly around each other. Like many of the 1997 designs, they were in an edition of 750. So were the 16 inch (40.5cm) Blueberry Bear, made from a beautiful textured mohair, and the 12 inch Chess, with his black and white chequered body, his half white/half black head, and with one black arm, leg and ear and one white one.

In spite of his dramatic colouring, the pattern for Chess was actually quite traditional, and the same was true of the Bear in a Bag. Measuring 10 inches (25.5cm) and fully jointed, he came in a brightly striped drawstring bag that matched the bold bow tie at his neck, and he was in an edition of 500.

Matching fabrics were a feature of the 12 inch (30.5cm) Little Joe too, but in his case the same tweed cloth was used on his pads and for the scarf around his neck. Little Joe himself was made from mohair in a bearish shade of brown, and he was again limited to just 500.

So was a much larger (20 inch/51cm) brown bear that was traditional in design but was fitted with a music mechanism. Round his neck was a ribbon on which was printed the words "Let me be your teddy bear".

Ebony and Ivory were two more classic bears in that size, each in an edition of 750 and in ebony and ivory shades. But the range also included some much smaller traditional-style teds. Ginger Nut and Banana Split, for instance, were made from sparse but luxurious fabrics that provided the inspiration for their names. Both measured 8 inches (20.5cm) and both were in editions of 500. Alexa, at 7 inches (18cm), was even smaller, and was in a pale shade of pink, with contrasting mohair used for her foot and paw pads, and with a lacy bow round her neck. She, too, was limited to 500.

An edition of the same size was selected for the new, smiling, Yes-No Bear Frazer, measuring twice Alexa's size and with mohair of a rich gingery shade. And another new design was John Axe's Ralph – measuring 15 inches (38cm) and in an edition of 1,000. A small head and long limbs were among his features.

The year's new offerings were completed by the 12 inch (30.5cm) Flossie, made from rich-brown mohair and

with extra-long limbs. A large head bow provided the finishing touch for this charmer, who was in an edition of 750.

There was no supplementary catalogue in 1997, but the International Collectors' Catalogue for 1998 was bigger than ever, with four extra pages and a huge range of styles and colours among the bears illustrated inside it. Again, there were a few old favourites, but by far the majority of the editions were brand-new designs or interesting variations on earlier themes, plus one or two replicas of classic teds to complete the picture.

Once again, Cheekys were very much in evidence, with eight new Micros (not counting the two in a swing boat), as well as some larger examples. One design that attracted particularly keen interest was the 8 inch

The 1998 Ancestor of Cheeky was based on the Punkinhead made for a Canadian department store from the late 1940s.

(20.5cm) Ancestor of Cheeky – with the same mohair topknot and colourful felt trousers (in this case red) as were seen on Cheeky's smiling predecessor, Punkinhead.

Other Cheeky items included a black and white set of two 8 inch (20.5cm) bears in an edition of 500, while the smaller Micros (measuring 6 inches/15cm) ranged from a

Cheeky Little Pharaoh and a sailor known as Cheeky Sails the Seven Seas, to a Cheeky Scent Bottle, whose head could be removed to reveal the container inside him. A chef (Cheeky Cordon Bleu), a white and silver Cheeky Arctic Angel, a pink Cheeky Golden Cherub, a bright red Cheeky Fire Glow and a multi-coloured Ice Cream Sundae completed the line-up of these small teds.

There were larger Cheeky Coral Blush bears in three sizes (15, 17 and 26 inches or 38, 43 and 66cm) as well – in a vibrant coral pink mohair – and also three Cheeky Golden Beans, with bean-filled tummies and in 8, 10 and 15 inch sizes (20.5, 25.5 and 38cm). In addition, the Cheeky was featured in two new bear-sized accessories – a Cheeky Back Pack and a Cheeky Mini Muff.

Other variations on previous designs included bright blue versions of the Ironbridge Bear in three sizes and another variant of the same bear in hessian, as well as a nutmeg-coloured Baby Baggy Bear in two sizes and a School Report Mischief, hiding his (no doubt poor) school report behind his back. There was a new brown Bearheart too, while replicas of a black Farnell bear (in three sizes) and of a turquoise Farnell (16 inches/40.5cm) also appeared, along with a Farnell nightdress case replica.

Among the brand-new offerings, on the other hand, was an exquisite Diana Bear – a tribute to Diana Princess of Wales, holding a hand-made rose in her paws – and there were five little Spice Bears in suitably spicy shades, complete with their own rack. Bright red mohair was used for the long-limbed Madam Butterfly, accessorized with Chinese brocade, while there was more fiery red in Ember The Fire Bear – one of four designs representing the elements. Neptune The Water Bear mirrored the colours of the oceans, while Rainbow The Air Bear was snowy white and Forest The Earth Bear a rich brown.

Totally different again were a farmer, known as Harvest Home, a Boating Bear in a sailor's tunic (and complete with toy boat), and the tassel-trimmed Tassels. The selection of gollies included a boxed bear and golly set as well as a half bear/half golly known as Upsy Daisy Golly/Bear, and among the other bears were the black Masked Ball and the bright red Masquerade – dressed in their evening finery, complete with masks.

The soulful Caught in the Rain, with his wet-look plush, was also new, as was a Dressage Bear on his own

The 1998 Diana Bear was a tribute to Diana Princess of Wales, and was in a limited edition of 2,500.

The 18 inch (45.5cm) Tassels was introduced in 1998, in an edition of 500.

The giant Baxter (left) was in an edition of just 100, while the Sloth Bear was limited to 250; both appeared in 1998.

mohair horse. Then there was Monty the Musical Bear, who played a tune at the turn of a key. Jingles and Jangles had large, jingly bells in their tummies, and there was a new Yes/No bear by the name of Ragamuffin. A 25 inch (63.5cm) Sloth Bear and the similarly sized Baxter, along with a smaller 14 inch (35.5cm) panda, were other new arrivals.

Later in the year, there were some additional lines for collectors in a special Autumn Premier brochure. Again, they included some Cheekys – three Cheeky Cocoa Bears, measuring 8, 10 and 15 inches (20.5, 25.5 and 38cm) and made from distressed cotton, as well as a Cheeky Little Mandarin (6 inches/15cm) and a snow-white Cheeky Snowflake measuring 8 inches (20.5cm).

A smiling Yes/No bear by the name of Bubbles and available in three sizes was another newcomer. So was the unusual Waggle Head, who had gangly limbs and a special wobbly head joint, and there was a giant 32 inch (81cm) version of the classic Magnet Bear in an edition of just 50.

In 1999, Merrythought prepared to celebrate the Millennium with a range of three bears (including a Cheeky and a Magnet) in a special amethyst-coloured mohair, along with a Millennium Golly. But there were also more Cheekys than ever. The Micros included a Cheeky Little Caveman, a Cheeky on Safari and a Cheeky

Little Panda, as well as a Cheeky Trick or Treat to celebrate Halloween, a Cheeky Spearmint, in mohair with a hint of green, a Cheeky Vanilla in mohair with a paler pile, and a Cheeky Blue Angel. Slightly larger, at 8 inches (20.5cm), were Cheeky Silken Tip and Cheeky Coffee Cream – both made from beautiful tipped mohairs – and a Cheeky Pot Pouree set which consisted of six bears in pastel shades. Cheeky Sweetheart was larger again, at 10 inches (25.5cm), while Cheeky Cotton Candy was available in three sizes (15 to 26 inches, or 38 to 66cm). There were three Cheeky Green Beans, too (8, 10 and 15 inches, or 20.5, 25.5 and 38cm), while Cheeky Polar, made from pure white alpaca, was offered in a single, giant, 26 inch size (66cm) and the Cheeky Jumbo Heavenly Blue (made from a navy-tipped, blue mohair) was even bigger, at 32 inches (81cm).

A Millennium Cheeky, a Millennium Golly and a Millennium Bear were all produced in editions of 2,000.

There were two new Twisty Cheekys, too – this time in a smaller size than before (8 inches/20.5cm) – and a Cheeky Ferris Wheel Set that included four Micro Cheekys. The Ancestor of Cheeky was represented by a

New Micro Cheekys in 1999 included (left to right) Cheeky Little Caveman, Cheeky on Safari and Cheeky Little Panda.

new Archive version measuring 10 inches (25.5cm) and a 6 inch (15cm) Micro Punkinhead, while the Cheekys were completed by a classic Replica Cheeky, which came with a copy of *The Magic of Merrythought* book.

Replica bears that year included a blue Merrythought Magnet bear and an Alpha Farnell Sunkissed Gold, as well as an Alpha Farnell Alpaca bear - and alpaca was also used for a new Yes/No Grizzly Bear, standing on all fours. The Standing Bruno - measuring an imposing 27 inches (68.5cm) and made from a tipped mohair - was likewise inspired by a real bear, while Polestar followed a visit to Canada by design director Jacqueline Revitt, who was entranced by the polar bears in Native Indian art there.

The inspiration for the Raccooba Bear, on the other hand, came from his unusual fluffy fabric, while a smudgy woven plush was used to make Pebbles, and a luxurious tipped plush was turned into a new Baby Baggy Bear Tipped. There was a smaller Baby Baggy Cub, too, in a soft alpaca, while a velvety fabric in shades of ginger and brown was used to create Smudge.

A shaggy, tipped mohair, on the other hand, was chosen for the new Banana Cream version of Waggle Head, while Ashley was in a deep midnight blue. Salt and pepper shades were turned into a boxed Salt and Pepper set. A tangy orange mohair was used for the new Ironbridge Bears, known as Orange Fizz, and a heavy brocade was just right for a special Bridal Bear to mark a special day.

There was a pure white New Born Bear, too, made from mohair, while totally different effects were achieved by using Ultra Suede for a bear of that name, and a soft kid leather for the shiny Leather Ted. Traditional mohair was used for the little Magnet Bear included in a Micro Mag and Golly Set, however, and mohair was also chosen

The 1999 Polestar, available in two sizes, followed a visit to Canada by designer Jacqueline Revitt.

This 1999 Salt and Pepper set came in its own presentation box.

for the vibrant Red Rascal Bear; a Red Rascal Golly was among the various new gollies on offer.

Once again, a supplementary catalogue was brought out later in the year. Several of the new bears offered in it were in limited editions. They included a suitably accessorized Explorer Bear in tipped mohair, as well as a Cheeky Little Darling with hearts on her footpad and ribbon, and two Cheeky Christmas ornaments – a Cheeky Snowman and a Cheeky Christmas Tree. There was a new, limited, Brandy Butter Magnet bear in three sizes as well, while a new Cheeky in three sizes (15 to 26 inches, or 38 to 66cm) was unlimited.

Two other unlimited designs had equal appeal for both children and collectors. The fully jointed Oak Leaf Bear, in four sizes, was made from mohair with an Oak Leaf embroidered on his left footpad, while the Beans 'n' Bears were in three sizes and had an inner bean-filled skin, so that they could be posed in many positions.

Both of these latter two designs appeared again in the year 2000 catalogue which, for the first time, combined both the toys and the collectors' editions in a single volume. That year, though, they were firmly placed among the designs for collectors, while a year later they had joined the designs aimed at all ages.

The range for collectors remained as wide as ever in the year 2000 combined catalogue, with the usual mix of brand-new designs, replicas, and new versions of old favourites. Once more there was an abundance of Cheekys.

A new Millennium Angel, in the form of a Cheeky, had joined the Millennium range from the previous year, for example, while the new Micros included a Cheeky Little Busy Bee, a Cheeky Little Ladybird and a Cheeky Little Sweep, as well as a Cheeky Easter Bunny wearing a bunny-ears bonnet. There were two Cheeky Little Jesters of the same size, and also two new Christmas ornaments – a Cheeky Christmas Bauble and a Cheeky Little Santa. Three more of these small Cheekys were riding in the Rocket to the Stars.

A Cheeky Beany Panda was made in the slightly larger 8 inch (20.5cm) size, and a new Mr & Mrs Twisty Cheeky Sunday Best were of similar height. The blue and pink Cheeky Baby Love, on the other hand, was available in three sizes (15 to 26 inches, or 38 to 66cm), and there were three sizes (8 to 15 inches, or 20.5 to 38cm) of the

143

Among the new Cheekys for 2000 were the festive Cheeky Christmas Bauble and Cheeky Little Santa.

These three replicas appeared in the 2000 catalogue, along with the original Farnells. Left to right: Pink Replica, Toffee and Freddie Farnell.

Cheeky Cool Kiwi Bean Bears, in an unusual, tipped, green mohair. Cheeky Naturally Linen, on the other hand, was in a single jumbo size of 32 inches (81cm).

An Ancestor of Cheeky was included in the Millennium Pledge Bears "Stardust" Range – all of which were in boxed limited editions but were also intended to be very special bears for a child to own. (A Magnet Stardust was another of the designs.) A further Ancestor of Cheeky – this time a Micro one – was among the four designs in a Commemorative Boxed Set released to mark 70 years of Merrythought. The remaining three were Micro versions of the 1930 Magnet Bear, the 1991 Jubilee Bear and the 1999 Millennium Bear.

There was a genuine replica of a 1930s Magnet Bear too, along with a new type of Magnet that had been updated for the year 2000. Three Farnells were replicated – among them Farnell's Toffee Bear, a well as a pink bear by the company and the 1930s Freddie Farnell that had been one of the stars of the BBC's *Antiques Roadshow*. There was a new version of the popular Mischief – this time a festive Mischief Dear Santa – and a bear-sized Mischief Backpack and Mischief Mini Muff replaced the previous little accessories.

The Millennium year catalogue featured a tribute to Her Majesty Queen Elizabeth the Queen Mother.

Capricorn was one of 12 Heavenly Bears, launched in 2000.

A totally new bear was created to celebrate Merrythought's 70th Anniversary, however, and other new designs that year included a tribute to Her Majesty Queen Elizabeth the Queen Mother, made from the palest green mohair. Then there were three that had been inspired by real bears - namely, the upright Serena The She Bear and her two cubs, Timber (Brown) and Forest (Cream). Different again were the 12 Heavenly Bears, representing the 12 signs of the Zodiac, and a boxed set of black and white Spirit Bears, inspired by a Canadian legend.

An upholstery velvet embossed with flowers was used for the Velvet Bear, offered in an edition of 500 in the year 2000.

Finally there were the lovable Smooch, with his bean-filled body, and two little 8 inch (20.5cm) bears named Whisky and Soda, as well as a fully jointed Velvet Bear, made from an upholstery velvet in a rich shade of red, embossed with flowers.

A supplementary catalogue brought a classic bear by the name of William, in three sizes, along with a 36 inch (91.5cm) standing Millionaire Teddy Bear and an 8 inch (20.5cm) Wedding Bear. There were also several new

New editions in 2001 included replicas of the 1960s Peter Bear (left) and a 1950s Teddy Bear (right), as well as Cheeky Spring Meadow (centre back) and a Circus Golly (centre front).

Cheeky-related items. Cheeky Amber Glow was available in three sizes, and there were the hooded Cheeky Little Puppy and Cheeky Little Kitty in two sizes, as well as a Jack-in-the-Box Cheeky. A Jack-in-the-Box Mischief and Jack-in-the-Box Golly were other new items.

In 2001, the bears for collectors and those intended for children were again contained in a single catalogue, but there was still a wide range of collectables, including a few from the previous catalogue together with many new introductions.

As usual, lovers of the Cheeky were well catered for. A 21st Century Cheeky, a pink Yes/No version, a Cheeky Bright Eyes, Cheeky Sweetheart (with heart-decorated, heart-shaped cushion) and Cheeky and His Best Friend Golly were just some of the designs. Cheeky High Society, in a shaggy gold mohair, was another new arrival, in three sizes, and there was a pair of Cheeky Carol Singers, as well as another Cheeky Christmas Bauble, a Cheeky Christmas Blessing, a Cheeky Little Reindeer, and

a green and red Festive Ancestor of Cheeky – not to mention the Cheeky Little Snowbear in his white hood.

Other hooded Cheekys were the Cheeky Little Tom Cat and the Cheeky Springtime Bunny, both of which were available in three sizes, and there were also three sizes for the more traditional Cheeky Barley Corn. The green Cheeky Spring Meadow, on the other hand, was in one, 32 inch (81cm) size, while others were in the form of 6 inch (15cm) Micros. They included a Cheeky Pas De Deux (in tutu), a Cheeky Tooth Fairy, the sleeping Cheeky in Dreamland, a Cheeky Little Bat and Cheeky Koala, while the Cheeky magician, known as Cheeky Abracadabra, was 2 inches (2.5cm) larger.

There were also five Flower Fairy Cheekys in the Micro size – sold as a set, complete with toadstool stand – as well as pink or blue panda-style Cheekys (Cheeky Pastel Panda Pink and Blue). Two Jack-in-the-Box versions of the Ancestor of Cheeky appeared, too, while another Cheeky was in the form of a Muff, complete with purse.

Two other popular Merrythought designs – Mischief and Wellington – had also been turned into Muffs, again with purses. Mischief appeared as the clown Pierrot too, while there was a new black version of Wellington, in three sizes.

Freddie Farnell, a Farnell replica from the previous year's catalogue, was likewise available in a new form – this time a 16 inch (40.5cm) version – and there were several replicas of early Merrythought designs. Peter Bear, for example, was first seen in the early 1960s, and was now available in three sizes, as was an unusual, standing, 1950s Teddy Bear which had never appeared in a Merrythought catalogue. A rare 1940s Bell Hop was reproduced as well.

To celebrate the centenary of the teddy bear, Merrythought introduced a range of Don't Shoot Bears, including a Jack-in-the-box version (left); the Theodore Bear (right) was based on early American ones.

A 21st Century Bear (left) and the Batik Bear were both introduced in 2001.

Other new designs for 2001 included the open-mouthed Smiler, along with a suitably dressed Rugby Player, a Batik Bear in batik-dyed mohair, a 21st Century Bear, a Wedding Pair, three Antique Pandas, and a long, lean Catwalk Bear, just crying out to be dressed in the latest fashions. There was also a pure white Little Treasure wearing a white bib that could be personalized with an embroidered name and date.

Later in the year, Merrythought brought out an unusually comprehensive additional catalogue. The year 2002 would mark the Centenary of the teddy bear, and the firm was keen to celebrate the event in fitting fashion with a whole collection of new designs. They included several Don't Shoot Bears, based on the real bear that appeared in a cartoon of American President Theodore (Teddy) Roosevelt in 1902. The picture showed Roosevelt refusing to shoot a captured cub – an event that would, in due course, lead to the teddy bear being named after him.

Merrythought's interpretations of the picture included a Yes/No bear and one in the form of a Jack in the Box. A special commemorative Theodore Bear 100 Years was also introduced – based on the early American teddies.

There were other traditional-style, jointed bears as well – among them the cotton plush Corn Pepper, the mohair Much Wenlock Bear and the mohair Sunshine Bear, which were each available in five sizes. A 13 inch (33cm) Antique Bear was in traditional gold, while six other classic designs – Galaxy, Taylor, Gordon, Musical Alex, Bruce and Humphrey – were all in small editions of just 100 (one bear for each year that the teddy had been in existence). The Sir John Harvey Jones Business Bear, on the other hand, was limited to 250, and was accessorized with a bright red tie.

Other new bears included 11 inch (28cm) jointed mohair versions of four of the Heritage Bears – the Beefeater, Policeman, Highlander and Guardsman – and a

The Shoulder to Shoulder set was produced in an edition of 500 in 2002, following the September 11 atrocities.

Bombardier Bear, Bombardier Cheeky and Bombardier Golly were all new in 2002.

winsome I Love You Eyes. But there were new Cheekys as well – among them the Cheeky Nectarine, in a vibrant, tangerine-coloured mohair, which was available in three sizes. Even more striking was a magnificent Cheeky Check Mate chess set, limited to just 25 – with each piece of the set in the form of a Cheeky bear. Then there were three mohair bags (two handbags and an evening bag) that were decorated with Cheeky heads, as well as a warmly dressed blue and white Cheeky Winter Wonderland bear.

Cheekys abounded in the 2002 catalogue as well, with more than six pages devoted to them. There were no fewer than six of them in the Cheeky Old Woman Who Lived in a Shoe set, and another eight in the Cheeky Princess & Her Little Helpers piece. Another two were Cheekys on a Picnic, while the new Micros included the vibrant Cheeky Mango, Cheeky Cranberry and Cheeky Lemon Fizz – each named after the colour of its mohair. A striking blue was used for the 26 inch (66cm) Cheeky in Tune, while a rich red created the Cheeky Winter Warmer – well wrapped up in a matching hat and scarf.

There were three new festive Cheekys as well – a new Cheeky Bauble, a Cheeky Bauble Snowman and a Cheeky Joy to the World – while the 8 inch (20.5cm) designs included a Cheeky Little Witch, a Cheeky Spell Bound (with his book of spells) and a Cheeky Mr Bones, dressed up as a skeleton. The smallest of the three versions of Cheeky Hot Spice was also that size, while the three sizes of Cheeky Jungle Drums – with animal-print bow – ranged from 15 inches (38cm) to 26 inches (66cm).

Cheeky Washed-N-Loved, on the other hand, was in a single 10 inch (25.5cm) size, and was made from a special fabric that looked as though it had taken a few turns in the washing machine. Cheeky Always and Forever consisted of two more Micro bears, and two Micro Cheekys were also used in the Cheeky Shoulder to Shoulder Set that was produced following the September 11 atrocities.

Cheeky novelties included three new bags decorated with Cheeky heads, as well as two Clutch purses carrying Cheeky motifs. There were three new Jack-in-

149

the-Box Cheekys (one of them a panda), and there were also five Cheeky Snuggle-Up cushions – in blue, red, white, lemon and gold. In addition, the new range featured no fewer than seven versions of Ancestor of Cheeky.

A Cheeky was one of two new bears created to celebrate the Golden Jubilee of Queen Elizabeth II too, and a Bombardier Cheeky was one of three "Bombardier" designs, inspired by the Bombardier Bruin of the 1930s. The others were a Bombardier Bear and a Bombardier Golly. A Cheeky Golly, with typically smiling face, could be found among the gollies.

Other new designs for the Centenary year included four bears representing the four seasons – MacWinter, Springtime Sprinkler, Rambling Rose and Woody – and there were special Mother's Day and Father's Day Bears (with "Best Mom" or "Best Dad" embroidered on a footpad). A St Nicholas bear and a Mischief Trick or Treat celebrated other annual festivals.

Me and My Chick, on the other hand, would have made an ideal Easter gift, with the egg motif on his footpad and the furry chick in his paws, while the Saver Bear was perfect for any collectors wanting to put aside funds for new acquisitions. On his footpad were pound, dollar and Yen signs, and he had with him his own Merrythought piggy bank.

The Dreamland Carousel was another new offering, and featured a bear riding a white carousel pony, while Vincent and Claude commemorated two renowned artists. There was a Confetti Bear, named after the black print fabric from which he was made, while Brambles was a distinctively curly, long-limbed ted, and little Titch was a shaggy fellow measuring a mere 7 inches (18cm).

Classic, fully-jointed bears, on the other hand, included Toby, in three sizes, and five versions of Dylan (the largest four with growls), as well as the 14 inch (35.5cm) Robby, Lester and Jerry. There were two Farnell replicas – the 26 inch (66cm) Winston and another 16 inch (40.5cm) ted produced as a Yes/No bear. Four Vintage Pandas joined the range, as did a Roly Poly Polar Bear in two sizes, and there were three sitting Hug-A-Bears, wearing contrasting T-shirts.

Comprehensive though the 2002 range was, there was once again a bumper Summer Catalogue a few months later, bringing a host of further new designs – among them traditional bears in four sizes and three new Magnets in a shaggy mohair. A beautiful Alpha Farnell, known as Alpha Farnell Cream Dream, joined the range, along with a Hat & Scarf Bear in red knitted accessories, while the celebrations of the Golden Jubilee continued with a Jubilee Bear and a Jubilee Cheeky - each carrying a small crown on a bright red cushion.

There were three new Ancestors of Cheeky, in shades of brown, along with the shaggy Chocolate Box Cheekys in Vanilla and Dark Chocolate. A Cheeky Raspberry Ripple was in a striking new tipped mohair, and Cheekys also turned up as a hooded Cheeky Kangaroo, as well as the Micro-sized Cheeky Cheetah Cub and Cheeky Little Graduate. There was a red, white and blue Cheeky True Brit too, with a patriotic Union Jack bow.

Other Cheeky-related designs included four Ancestors of Cheeky - a Yes/No version, a Clown and a colourful Pure Pink Punk, along with a coordinating Ancestor of Cheeky and Golly "Old Town" set. There were also two blue and white Christmas designs – known as Cheeky Crystal Christmas and Ancestor of Cheeky Christmas.

Pink and Blue Baby Bears, a vibrant Berry Red Ted, a tartan-bowed Mac Bear and a little Christmas Stocking Bear were other new designs. So was the Cyril Centenary bear, designed by John Axe, while a teddy-decorated Picnic Set, Loving Cup and Piggy Bank rounded off the final Merrythought catalogue for the Centenary year.

Chapter 11

11. SPECIALS: UK

For collectors hoping to identify a Merrythought bear, one of the major problems is that so many of the firm's designs are never included in any of their catalogues. Some appear to have been extra lines, introduced after the catalogue went to press perhaps, or possibly simply added to the firm's stand at a trade show to see what the response would be. But others have been made exclusively for an individual customer, such as one of the major London department stores.

Unfortunately, information about them in the company's archives is often sketchy or even totally non-existent. If the design in question was a brand-new one, there might be details of it in the firm's Trials Books, that itemize each new development. But the books do not generally indicate whether or not the new creations were intended for specific shops or chains. And just because something was entered in the books does not mean that it ever went into production.

Often, the only evidence that such items were actually made is in the memories of the people who worked for Merrythought at the time. But with so many lines being made over the years, few people can remember the details of any specific exclusives (hardly surprising when the numbers made would, in many cases, have been very small).

It was only in 1992 that the firm began keeping some kind of record of every single variation on its designs – but even today the information is far from complete. Although there is often mention of the store or distributor for whom the bears were intended, it is not always clear whether or not they ever went into production. Descriptions are far from complete

The bear on the left was one of the TS bears made for Harrods, and dates from the late 1980s; that on the right was made for the House of Fraser around the same time.

(although a coded numbering system does give some clues), and in most cases there are no indications as to the sizes of any limited editions. A few are remembered by those involved with them at the time, but again, as with the earlier examples, information is often frustratingly sketchy.

This chapter, and the following one, can therefore only dip into the vast array of such designs that have appeared over the years. The coverage relies heavily on information contained in the catalogues produced by some of the firm's distributors and by certain shops, as well as anecdotal information from collectors and from Merrythought employees. As a result these pages can, with just a handful of exceptions, cover only designs from the last 20 years or so – and only some of the many hundreds that have appeared in that time.

Many special Merrythoughts have been made for major department stores – among them Harrods, Selfridges, John Lewis and Debenhams. But these bears have often simply carried the usual Merrythought label,

Various special Cheekys have been made for London department store Harrods. This one dates from the mid 1990s.

The Whirled Mohair Original Teddy Bear was made for Harrods in the 1980s in a boxed, limited edition of 1,000.

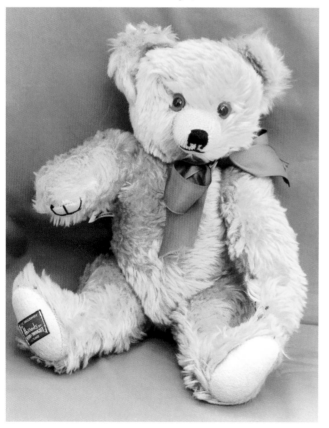

and it can therefore be extremely hard to identify them as exclusives. Some have simply been variations on items in the regular Merrythought range – made in different fabrics perhaps, or in a different size – but there have been totally original designs as well. A few bears that first saw the light of day as a shop exclusive were later made available on a wider scale, in another form.

Certainly, the firm was making special bears for Harrods long before it began keeping records of them, and well before the special Merrythought Harrods label was introduced in the 1980s. By then there was a whole range of what were known as Harrods TS Bears, in a wide range of sizes. Many early collectors were tempted to acquire one, since traditional, fully jointed mohair bears were so hard to find at that time. These had shaved muzzles and distinctive nose stitching, reminiscent of that of many early Merrythought teds.

Of even greater interest to collectors, however, was the Whirled Mohair Original Teddy Bear – which came in a Harrods green box and was limited to just 1,000. The

This plush, bean-filled bear was bought from Harrods in the late 1980s, and has the green Harrods Merrythought label on his back.

description on the box included the information that he was made from an original 1930s pattern – which in fact was that which today is widely known as the Magnet Bear. The fabric, too, was said to be at least 30 years old, with its distinctive finish the result of a special "whirling brush process".

Some time later, the same fabric was used for an exclusive Harrods Cheeky, with a shaved nose. He was one of many special Cheekys that have been made for the store over the years. A special woven fabric was chosen for his pads, but Merrythought quickly abandoned its use after it was discovered that it had a tendency to deteriorate over time.

In 1988, a special little bean-filled bear in bright yellow plush was produced very much with children rather than collectors in mind, and a year later a Merrythought version of the Harrods Doorman was introduced. With his head, paws and feet made from mohair, he was similar to the Heritage Bears that were

included in Merrythought's regular range – but the doorman's smart uniform in the distinctive Harrods green was totally unique.

When tipped mohairs started to appear, some Harrods bears were soon being made in that cloth as well – again attracting the interest of collectors as well as those wanting a special gift for a child. Then, in the early 1990s, an Attic Bear in an unusual curly plush was also produced as a Harrods exclusive. Not long afterwards, the first Attic Bear appeared in the International Collectors' Catalogue.

Another Harrods exclusive was a Mother and Baby set – the baby being a traditional 5 inch (12.5cm) miniature with a Harrods green bow. And in 1991, a dark brown Dr Italian was created for a special Italian promotion in the store; he came complete with a striking velvet hat, cloak and sash. Dressed bears were not popular at the time,

Merrythought began making the Harrods Doorman in the late 1980s; his head, paws and feet are all mohair.

A long and lean Attic Bear was made for Harrods before other versions went on sale worldwide.

Dr Italian was created in the early 1990s to coincide with a special Italian promotion in Harrods; many examples were eventually sold undressed.

however, and eventually the bears were offered for sale without their costumes, making the costumed versions even more of a rarity.

A traditional gold Harrodian Bear went on sale a year or two later – measuring a substantial 20 inches (51cm) – and a string of other specials have followed. In 1998, for example, there was Golden Paws in a luxury curled mohair, with golden pads and bow. In 1999 came the bean-filled, 8 inch (20.5cm) Coffee Bean Bear, and other exclusives have included small mohair replicas of each of the Harrods Christmas bears since the late 1990s.

Harrods is by no means the only major store to have commissioned its own Merrythought lines, however. Large numbers of Cheeky nightdress cases were made for John Lewis in the 1960s and 1970s, for example – both in mohair and in various synthetic plushes. Like many of the later exclusives, however, they had no special label to distinguish them from other Merrythought lines.

Later designs for this retailer included some brown plush bears in the early 1990s, followed soon afterwards by some slim little mohair bears whose ribbons in the John Lewis colours of green and white were the only clues to the exclusivity of the design. Eventually, though, some Merrythought bears were produced with John Lewis's own Mischief label on one of their foot pads, as well as the manufacturer's swing tag, and a Merrythought cloth tag stitched into a side seam. A slim, jointed Millennium Bear, made for the toy department from a fairly long mohair and in an open edition, has been one of the other John Lewis exclusives.

Back in the late 1980s there were some long-armed, very traditional bears that were available only through the House of Fraser stores, and some other traditional teds were sold only by Selfridges. That firm's 1990 Christmas catalogue, for example, shows a golden yellow ted based on a 1930s design, and two years later there was another traditional bear, with the long paws and

ABOVE: *Giant (26 inch/66cm) Cheeky nightdress cases were made for John Lewis in a wide variety of fabrics during the 1960s and 1970s.*

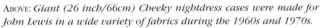

TOP RIGHT: *This 12 inch (30.5cm) mohair bear with brocade pads was bought from John Lewis in 1993; his ribbons are in the store's colours.*

BOTTOM RIGHT: *This mohair bear, carrying the John Lewis Mischief label, was bought in 1993.*

large feet of the early 20th century (long before Merrythought was founded).

Selfridges also offered some exclusive bears in synthetic plush at around this time. They included a fully jointed ted in a coppery shade, as well as a plump, champagne-coloured one that was unjointed to make him extra cuddly.

More recently a number of different designs were devised by Merrythought for the Debenhams chain, but it is not only department stores that have commissioned their own designs. Toy shops, too, have sometimes offered them. The Gamley chain, based in the south of England, had a Merrythought bear known as Gamley in

ABOVE: *This fully jointed mohair bear was made in a boxed, limited edition of 1,000 for Hamleys in the late 1980s. He is similar in design to the Ironbridge Bears.*

TOP LEFT: *A number of special bears have been produced for Selfridges; this mohair example dates from around the late 1990s.*

BOTTOM LEFT: *The unjointed Gamley was produced for the toy shops of the same name in the 1980s.*

the mid-1980s – dressed in blue denim dungarees with a red and white G logo on the front.

Others have been produced for Hamleys in London's Regent Street. They have ranged from traditional, fully jointed toys in synthetic plush or mohair to special editions for collectors – such as an exclusive Dancing Bear and a special version of the Love in a Mist pair from the 1997 Merrythought catalogue. A boxed, limited-edition, traditional bear was produced in the late 1980s.

Other special Merrythoughts have turned up in more unexpected places. Jointed bears in various sizes have been made for Burberry, for example – with the famous Burberry checked fabric used for their pads and bow ties. A Burberry golfer bear, similar to those in the

Merrythought has been making jointed bears for Burberry since the late 1980s or early 1990s. Burberry fabric is used for the pads and bow tie.

A synthetic plush was used to make this 10 inch (25.5cm) bear for Collier Campbell; the interior design company's own fabric was used for the pads, ear linings and bow tie.

Heritage range, but again with Burberry fabric used in his costume, also appeared for a while in the early 1990s. Some of these bears had only a Burberry label, with no mention of Merrythought on either the bears themselves or any boxes they came in. But since they were made from regular Merrythought patterns they were easy to identify.

So, too, were some little jointed bears made for the London-based interior design company Collier Campbell, around the early 1990s. Again the firm's own fabric was used for the pads and bow tie, and in this case for the ear linings as well. No doubt, other firms commissioned their own variants too, but today there is no record of them.

A number of other designs have been sold by mail order – through Lawleys by Post, for example, and through Compton & Woodhouse. Lawleys by Post offerings have included a Four Seasons Teddy Collection, made up of Easter Parade (in Easter bonnet), Beach Belle

(with sun hat and beach towel), Windy Days (with jaunty peaked cap and wind-blown umbrella) and Frosty Winter (in red and white scarf and hat set). *Now I lay me down to sleep*, on the other hand, was kneeling with his paws held together in prayer; he wore a nightcap and carried his own hot water bottle, and was again part of a four-bear series representing different times of the day.

The Compton & Woodhouse designs have likewise been exceptionally varied. Bruno, for example, was an official RSPCA Collector's Bear, and came with his own little dog by the name of Puddles. The first bear in the edition was auctioned in aid of the charity, and a donation was made for each bear that was sold.

Then there was Visiting Day, which supported the Great Ormond Street Hospital Children's Charity. Made from mohair in the palest shade of silvery grey, he carried a posy of hand-sewn flowers. Others have included the Pandamonium panda, which helped to raise funds for the Born Free Foundation.

Another design for Compton & Woodhouse was a champagne-coloured Auld Lang Syne Bear, limited to 1999 and with that year embroidered on its left foot, to celebrate the New Year in 1999. A Christmas Bear later that year was made from old gold mohair with a Royal Stewart bow tie, and with the year and a sprig of holly embroidered on its foot.

Other Christmas and New Year Bears followed. Hogmanay was the Merrythought New Year's Eve Bear 2000, for example – made from cream mohair with a tartan tam-o'shanter and sash and again with the year embroidered on the left foot. Later that year there was the quite different Class of 2000 – limited to production

in the year 2000. He wore a striped school tie and carried a brown leather satchel.

The same year also saw the hazelnut-coloured Merrythought Heirloom Bear of the Year 2000 – a very traditional ted, known as Edward and with the year 2000 embroidered on his left foot. He was followed by William, the Merrythought Heirloom Bear of the Year 2001 (again with the year embroidered on the left foot), and the following year there was an Official Merrythought Golden Jubilee Bear 2002, wearing a sash and a gold-plated crown, and with the official Golden Jubilee crest embroidered on the left foot.

Another Merrythought design for Compton & Woodhouse was a Teddy Bears' Picnic bear, complete with tablecloth and two napkins as well as a basket

Compton & Woodhouse's Teddy Bears' Picnic has his own picnic basket and tea set and is limited to 2,450.

Bruno, one of the Compton & Woodbouse Charity Bear Collection, has his own little dog Puddles. The set is in a limited edition of 9,500.

The inspiration for Compton & Woodbouse's Freddie Fisher was a watercolour by Leigh Beavis-West. The bear was in an edition of 9,500.

Thruppence Bear wears a genuine threepenny bit round his neck; he is one of a whole series of Money Bears made for Compton & Woodbouse.

containing tiny cups, saucers, plates, tea pot, milk jug and sugar bowl - all made from porcelain - together with stainless steel cutlery.

Different again was Freddie Fisher, inspired by a Leigh Beavis-West watercolour. He wore blue dungarees and a straw hat, just like that in the picture. Then there was a whole series of Money Bears, made in traditional colours of mohair and with original, pre-decimalization coins mounted in gold-plated sterling silver. Farthing, Ha'penny, Penny, Thruppence, Sixpence and Shilling were the first six designs - each with a Union Jack incorporated in the Merrythought label affixed to the right foot, and the bear's name embroidered on the left one.

Two other bears, Holly and Cookie, were designed to sit on the edges of the bookends that were given away free to those buying the pair. Both were dressed in pale blue outfits - Holly in a dress with a frill at the hem made from a dark blue checked fabric, and Cookie in dungarees with straps and a pocket in the same checked fabric.

Compton & Woodhouse are not the only ones to have used special Merrythought bears to raise money for charity. A traditional jointed ted, based on one owned by Dame Judi Dench, was sold in aid of The Child Psychotherapy Trust, of which Dame Judi was a Vice Patron. Sixteen special Merrythought bears, dressed by leading designers, were auctioned in aid of the NSPCC at Christie's in 1998, and a number of other one-of-a-kind creations have likewise been sold at the auction house in aid of other charities.

In 1994, for example, a beautiful Mother and Baby Cheeky, under the name There There Little Bear, was sold in aid of the BBC Children in Need Appeal. A year later, a tipped mohair ted with distinctive "chapel window"

A special label on the foot of this mohair bear shows that it was made specially for Asquiths; it dates from around the late 1980s.

claws on his paws and feet raised money for the British Red Cross "Youth", and in 1996 proceeds from the 26 inch (66cm) Big Blue, with similar claw stitching, went to the Save the Children Fund.

By then, specialist teddy bear shops had begun to appear all over Britain, and some of them had commissioned their own exclusive designs from Merrythought too. In the late 1980s, for example, Merrythought made a beautiful, traditional bear for Asquiths, and his place was later taken by Lofty, which has remained on sale for many years.

Merrythought has made Lofty for the Asquiths bear shops for many years.

A large number of other designs have been created for Teddy Bears of Witney, starting in 1991 with Barnaby – a replica of a 1930s bear on permanent display in the shop. Made from a long pile, faded gold mohair, he was limited to 600. At first he was sold undressed, but the

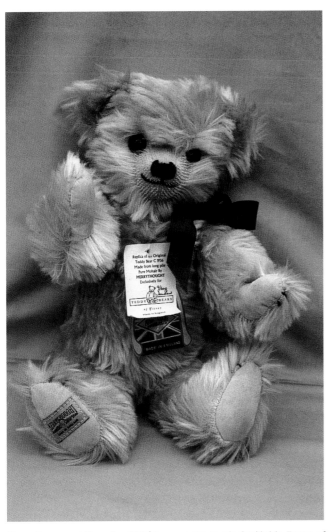

Barnaby - a replica of a 1936 bear - was made for Teddy Bears of Witney in a limited edition of 600.

1992-3 catalogue offered him in a Guernsey jumper embroidered with his name, and this version reappeared in 1996, while in 1995 he was available in a clown suit made from a Liberty fabric. The bare bear remained on sale at the same time, however.

By 1992 the shop also had its own version of the long-limbed Attic Bear, made from a distressed mohair and in what was then an exceptionally small limited edition of just 100. Then, in the 1996 catalogue, the first exclusive Witney Cheeky was launched. Measuring 15 inches (38cm), he was made from a distressed mohair with a soft pellet filling, and was again limited to just 100.

Other exclusive Witney Cheekys followed. The 1998 catalogue introduced a further pellet-filled version, this

time made from a bright red mohair and in an edition of 250. A year later, Mistletoe Cheeky arrived - in a rich shade of green with matching paw pads and with an off-white velveteen muzzle and feet. A sprig of mistletoe was embroidered on the left foot of the bear, which was this time limited to 500.

Witney Cheeky Bean was softly filled and made in an edition of 250 for Teddy Bears of Witney in 1998.

A year later, it was time for the bright blue Cheeky Jack - a softly stuffed bear, made to celebrate the year 2000. He had a white muzzle and bright red pads, with a Union Jack on the left foot, and round his neck was a patriotic red, white and blue bow. The size of the edition was increased, appropriately, to 2000 to mark the special occasion.

The luxurious Cheeky Heart of Gold was introduced the same year, in a beautiful, long-pile alpaca with damask foot pads. He wore a gold waistcoat and gold bow tie, on which two interwoven bears had been embroidered. The number in this edition was just 250.

The 10.25 inch (26cm) Cheeky William appeared at that time too. He was a smaller version of a 26 inch (66cm), one-of-a-kind bear made by Merrythought and auctioned in aid of the shop's chosen charity (The Salvation Army) after Teddy Bears of Witney was voted Retailer of the Year by members of the Merrythought International Collectors' Club. It was the third year in succession that the shop had received this accolade. The smaller William, made from a sparse, grey-green mohair, was limited to 500, and a donation was made to the charity for each bear sold.

New Witney Cheekys for 2001 were Cheeky Robin Hood, in a green felt costume, and the festive Cheeky White Christmas, with a fur-trimmed red hat and matching bow tie – both limited to 250. Two rose-coloured Cheeky Little Kittens, with wired tails and removable bonnets, also appeared that year – one a Micro-sized 6 inches (15cm) and the other 10 inches (25.5cm) in height.

Two black and white Cheeky Lucky Kittens joined them a year later, as did three Cheeky Old Beans, made from a shaggy, long-pile, beige mohair, and three Cheeky Barley Corns in a luxurious gold mohair with cream velveteen pads. There was a Cheeky Aviator too, in old-fashioned helmet, goggles and scarf, as well as two exclusive Cheeky Shoulder Bags – one in the shape of a Cheeky bear's head, and the other in the form of a brown mohair bag with a gold Cheeky head attached two it.

In 2000, the shop had again been voted Retailer of the Year by members of the Merrythought International Collectors' Club, and this time a 26 inch (66cm) Pinkie Punkie – a sister for the ever-popular Punkinhead – was auctioned to help fund a nurse for Macmillan Cancer Relief. Two smaller versions – measuring 10 inches (25.5cm) and 6 inches (15cm) – were included in the Witney shop's 2002 catalogue, with the larger of the two bears in an edition of 500 and the Micro-sized one limited to 250. Again, a donation was made to the same charity for each bear sold.

Two more exclusive Punkinheads were included in the following year's catalogue. Witney Punkie was made from a swirled ginger mohair, with off-white tummy and brown-tipped topknot, and his red shorts had the name Witney embroidered on them. So did the brown ones

worn by his brother, Witney Golden Punkie, who was created from a pale gold mohair, with a cream tummy and again a tipped mohair topknot.

The 2003 Witney catalogue also included a whole clutch of new Witney Cheekys. The All Black Bean Cheeky was, as his name suggests, made from a black mohair, and had a pellet filling in his body. Cheeky Witney Rose, on the other hand, was a delicate shade of pink, with a white muzzle and pads – as was the smaller Cheeky Little Princess, who was given a pearl-edged, white silk cape and matching tiara.

Cheeky Little Prince, on the other hand, was in a swirled gold mohair, and wore a dramatic royal blue velour cape, trimmed with imitation ermine. Then there was Witney Blanket Cheeky, made from a pure wool blanket cloth, woven in the town of Witney itself, which is famous for such fabrics. The theme was also continued in his brown felt waistcoat, which was edged with blanket stitching. That same year, a brooch in the form of a Cheeky bear's head, made from gold mohair and complete with the familiar bells in the ears, was also introduced.

Not all the Witney exclusives of recent years have been Cheekys, however. When the shop was first voted Retailer of the Year by members of the Merrythought International Collectors Club, Merrythought made a special, one-of-a-kind bear which was sold in aid of the Helen House Hospice in Oxford. A smaller version of the 26 inch (66cm) Helen, measuring 12 inches (30.5cm) was sold by the shop (with a donation being made to the same charity for each bear sold). Known as Helen, she was created from a wavy, pale apricot mohair, tipped with brown.

A Witney Farnell has also been made by Merrythought – a replica of a c.1930s Farnell known as Didcock, on permanent display in the shop. A tousled mohair gives him a well-hugged look, just like that of the original.

No other British specialist shop has commissioned exclusive Merrythoughts in anything like the numbers produced for Teddy Bears of Witney, but several have offered one or two special designs. The Unique shop, which was based in Broadway, sold a copy of the dressed Bed-time Bear – a Cheeky that appeared in the 1977 Merrythought soft toy catalogue – while Bear with Us in Lichfield asked Merrythought to re-create two old

ABOVE: *The Unique shop in Broadway added a hot water bottle to its replica of the 1977 Bed-time Bear.*

TOP RIGHT: *Merrythought produced replicas of two Chad Valley bears for Bear with Us in Lichfield; they were available separately or as a set.*

RIGHT: *Dolly Land in London commissioned replicas of a 1932 Merrythought bear in three colours.*

Chad Valley teds for them. Dolly Land, in London's Winchmore Hill, on the other hand, commissioned replicas of the open-mouthed Laughing Baby Bears that appeared in the 1932 Merrythought catalogue. The modern versions were available in black, brown or white.

A group of shops known as Teddy's, and with branches at London airports, also had some designs made specially for them – including a fully jointed plush ted as well as an unusual creation in a shaggy blond mohair, of which just a handful were produced. But Arundel Teddy Bears in Sussex opted for a special Cheeky in a pale beige mohair, and another, in a short-pile plush, was made for Teddy's of Birmingham, which also had branches in Manchester, Stratford-upon-Avon, Bath and Chester. They sold their own traditional, fully jointed Merrythought bear as well, made from mohair.

In the late 1990s, Merrythought made some exclusive plush Cheekys for Teddy's of Birmingham and its sister shops.

This fully jointed plush bear was on sale at the Teddy's shops, at London's airports.

Bears on the Square, a short walk from the Merrythought factory in Ironbridge, have had a family of fully jointed plush bears made for them, and a number of special editions have been produced for the Ironbridge Gorge Museum Teddy Bear Shop, which is situated right next to the Merrythought factory's gates. Ironbridge George, for example, was dressed as a Victorian

workman, while Smithy wore an ultrasuede apron, and Jack the Printer's Apprentice (also in an apron) carried a list of apprenticeship rules in his paw.

The same shop has sold some special Merrythought Christmas bears too, including Holly in two sizes in 1998 (made in the darkest of green plushes) and the Jingles Celebration Bear a year later, made from a golden tipped mohair to mark the Millennium as well as the festive season.

Other special bears on sale in Ironbridge itself have been those produced especially for the Merrythought International Collectors' Club Open Days, held each July in and around the factory, but these will be covered in the chapter devoted to the club and the bears produced for its members.

A number of exclusives, including Smithy, have been produced for the Ironbridge Gorge Museum Teddy Bear Shop, which is situated next to the factory.

Compton & Woodhouse

Founded in 1985, Compton & Woodhouse have built up, over the years, an unrivalled reputation as specialists in the creation of fine collectibles. From their earliest days they worked only with the premier English potteries – Royal Doulton, Royal Crown Derby, Royal Worcester, Coalport and Wedgwood – and with the very best designers and sculptors throughout Europe.

Constantly pushing forward the boundaries of both design and quality, they created highly detailed fine bone china figurines as diverse in subject as fairytale figures like Sleeping Beauty, elegant Edwardian fashion figures correct in every authentic period detail, spectacular modern dance figures and appealing child studies, the latter often connected with a children's charity such as the NSPCC. At an early stage, they also diversified into other collectibles, still mainly in fine china – commemorative jugs, heirloom plates, prestigious anniversary pieces.

Then in 1999 came an exciting new development – the prospect of the first Compton & Woodhouse teddy bear. Following their tradition of only working with the very best craftsmen and artists in every field, the company was delighted to collaborate with Merrythought of England on this first bear. It was a suitably significant occasion. The Millennium Bear was issued in a strictly limited edition of 2,000 to celebrate the arrival of the 21st century – and as it turned out, herald an enduring partnership between Merrythought and Compton & Woodhouse.

More bears followed. A Royal Celebration, issued to mark the Queen's Golden Jubilee, swiftly sold out. The Money Bears, each with an example of the old, pre-decimal coinage and suitably named 'Sixpence', 'Thruppence' etc. were also best-selling bears.

The charity link, so long established, continued with bears issued in connection with the World Society for Animals (WSPA), particularly appropriate in view of that charity's long-running campaign, Libearty, to rescue bears in the wild. The Great Ormond Street Bear paid tribute to the magnificent work of the famous children's hospital and reminded us all of the enduring importance of a teddy bear as the first faithful friend and comforter of children. And not just children: Millie, the first Breast Cancer Care bear, came complete with the charity's trademark pink ribbon.

Other favourites along the way include the irresistible Evacuee Bear, clutching his little suitcase, and Holly and Cookie, a fetching twosome who proved resoundingly that the only thing better than one teddy bear is two teddy bears! The Coronation Bear, meanwhile, celebrated the 50th anniversary of the Queen's Coronation and incorporated an original Coronation Crown, first minted in 1953 and sought-after in its own right by coin collectors.

Most recently, the company was pleased to be invited to share in a longstanding Merrythought tradition with the announcement of the first Compton & Woodhouse 'Cheeky' bear. Cheeky bears are a particularly distinctive species of Merrythought bear – unique designs which have been created by Merrythought since 1957. The issue of Cheeky Prince Charming in 2003 sees the relationship between Compton & Woodhouse and Merrythought entering yet another exciting phase.

Chapter 12

12. SPECIALS: INTERNATIONAL

Many bears have been produced specially for individual Merrythought distributors, each of which represents the firm in a specific country or area. In fact, as we have already seen, America's Tide-Rider played a major role in the creation of the first Merrythought designs to be made specifically with collectors in mind. When the first of the International Collectors' Catalogues appeared in 1991, the creation of designs exclusively for distribution in the United States halted for a while. But in recent years, Tide-Rider has again been commissioning a whole range of editions that are on sale only in the United States.

In 1996, for example, American magazines carried advertisements for the fully jointed Cupcake and Honeybun, each measuring 9 inches (23cm) in height. Cupcake wore a yellow shirt and matching hat, with dungarees in a contrasting print fabric, while Honeybun had accessories in the same material, along with a wooden honey dipper in his paw.

There were three special Micro Cheekys that year as well – Cheeky Goes West, complete with ten-gallon hat and lasso; Cheeky 49'er, with hat and duffel bag; and Cheeky Gets His Man, in the form of a Canadian Mountie. All measured 6 inches (15cm). In addition, there was an 8 inch (20.5cm) version of Cheeky on Parade – which had appeared in a Micro version (6 inches/15cm) in the 1995 International Collectors' Catalogue. Each of the bears was limited to 250.

There were more special Tide-Rider Micro Cheekys in 1997 – this time including Cheeky Pocahontas in native American style, as well as Cheeky South of the Border in a white felt poncho, trimmed with green, red and gold. He wore a straw hat on his head and carried a basket of flowers in his paws. There was a Cheeky Ace Aviator, too, in leather bomber jacket and matching pilot's helmet, along with a white silk scarf, while the range was completed by Cheeky Workin' on the Railroad, in traditional blue and white striped overalls and hat, with a red bandanna round his neck and a red lantern in his paw. Again, all measured 6 inches (15cm) and were limited to 250.

Four other 1997 Tide-Rider exclusives were similarly limited. Red was a re-creation of an Alpha Farnell – made

in a black-tipped red mohair and measuring 16 inches (40.5cm). The 20 inch (51cm) Bear, on the other hand, re-created the one (also believed to be by Farnell) that was given to Christopher Robin Milne on his first birthday in 1921, and that was later immortalized in A.A. Milne's stories of Winnie-the-Pooh.

Also relatively traditional was the similarly sized Rocky, made from stone-coloured mohair, while the range was completed by two "Chums" – an 11 inch (28cm) bear with an 8 inch (20.5cm) golly backpack.

There were three more Farnell replicas for Tide-Rider a year later. The 20 inch (51cm) Cranberry took his name from the vibrant shade of his mohair, while the same-sized Barnet was in a more traditional gold, and reproduced a ted that was first seen around 1926. Another gold mohair was used for the smaller Little Bear – a 16 inch (40.5cm) brother for the Bear of the previous

Cranberry was a 20 inch (51cm) replica of an early Farnell, and was made exclusively for Tide-Rider in the USA in 1998.

Little Bear was a smaller brother for Bear; both were made for Tide-Rider, Merrythought's American distributor.

A Cheeky and Ancestor of Cheeky Backpack set were made for Tide-Rider in the USA in 1998.

year. Cranberry and Barnet were both limited to 250, while the edition size for Little Bear was increased to 500.

The Cheeky and Ancestor of Cheeky Backpack set that year was also in an edition of 500. It comprised a 12 inch (30.5cm) mohair Cheeky with a 7 inch (18cm) backpack in the form of an Ancestor of Cheeky, complete with mohair topknot. A 16 inch (40.5cm) version of the cuddly Baby Baggy Bear, in a rich brown mohair, was also on offer to American collectors, in an edition of just 250.

Another Baby Baggy Bear, this time measuring just 10 inches (25.5cm) and known as Baby Baggy Love, appeared in 1999. He was made from a pure white mohair with brown mohair accents (including ear linings and muzzle), and was again in an edition of 250. So, too, was Golden Glimmer, made from a luxuriously long and curly mohair and measuring 16 inches (40.5cm), and there were the same number of boxed Edwardian Bears

Golden Glimmer, made from a luxurious, textured mohair, was produced in an edition of 250 for Tide-Rider.

– smaller (10 inches/25.5cm) versions of Tide-Rider's first U.S.A. exclusive by Merrythought (see *A new direction*).

There were more new Alpha Farnells for Tide-Rider that year as well. The blond Biscuit was made in two sizes, namely 20 inches (51cm) and 16 inches (40.5cm) in editions of 100 and 150 respectively. The 26 inch (66cm) Berkley, made from a long-pile brown mohair, was an exact replica of an original Farnell in the Merrythought archives, and limited to 250. Then there was Lavender Blue. Made from an unusual blue mohair, he measured 16 inches (40.5cm) and was again limited to 250.

The Titanic Rescue Bear, made for the USA, wore a whistle round his neck, identical to that issued to the First Mate on the fated vessel.

Another new design that year was the Titanic Rescue Bear, wearing a cap and collar that replicated those worn by the First Mate on the Titanic, which sank in 1912. Round the bear's neck was an Acme Thunderer Whistle. It was identical to that issued to the first mate, which is

believed to have helped to save 700 lives when the vessel went down.

Totally different again was the Museum Magnet Bear – a 15 inch (38cm) replica of an early Merrythought that appeared on the cover of *The Magic of Merrythought* book (2nd printing). A copy of the book was offered free with the bear, which was limited to 500.

Holiday Cheeky Cherubs in red, as here, or green were among the Micro Cheekys made for the USA in 1999.

There were some new exclusive Cheekys in 1999 as well. Four 6 inch (15cm) Micros, known as Orange Whip, Ember, Strawberry Cream and Lemonade, all took their names from the beautiful mohairs used to make them. Two Holiday Cheeky Cherubs were the same size – one red and one green – and these were given gold leatherette pads, along with gold wings and a gold halo. At 8 inches (20.5cm), Ice Cream Sundae was slightly larger, and was created from three different mohairs in suitable shades, but his edition size was the same, at 250.

Three different shades of mohair were used for Ice Cream Sundae – an edition of 250 made for the USA.

Exclusive Cheekys appeared in the Millennium year, too – among them a special Cheeky 2000. He had cloisonné eyes with a sterling silver trim, and with a silver star in the pupils, as well as a special Year 2000 wishbone embroidered on his footpad. Made from a shaggy, sparse, beige mohair, he measured 8 inches (20.5cm) and was in an edition of 250.

The Lavender Blue Cheeky and Cheeky Be Mine were similar in size – the former taking his name from the colour of his mohair and the latter from the red embroidered heart, complete with Cupid's arrow, on his right footpad. Again, both were limited to 250.

Also limited to 250 were another four exclusive Micro Cheekys. One was another Holiday Cheeky Cherub, this time in cream mohair, while a Cheeky Father Time celebrated the coming of the new millennium. He was given a long white beard, made from mohair, and carried a sickle with 2000 emblazoned on it. A Cheeky Y2K Bug

was Merrythought's own millennium bug, made from green and gold mohair with gold pads and complete with antennae. And the Cheeky Little Monkey was equipped with an armature in his tail so that he could "hang out" with all the other Cheekys.

A new Tide-Rider Signature Series was also launched – the first designs being an 8 inch (20.5cm) Edwardian Bear in a red and blue waistcoat (signed by Merrythought Managing Director Oliver Holmes), and a Master Mischief in the same size (signed by Merrythought designer Jacqueline Revitt). There was no catapult hidden behind the back of this new Mischief, though; in its place was a bunch of felt flowers. Both designs were limited to 250.

So too was the very different Wishbone Logo Bear – a classic, fully jointed, 16 inch (40.5cm) bear with a dramatic red, white and blue bow. He came with a special Merrythought wishbone sign, making him an ideal addition to a whole collection of Merrythought bears.

Then there was the first *totally original* design to be created by Merrythought under the Alpha Farnell label. There were two versions of it – Tipped Davidson and Sunshine Davidson – named after the newest member of the Smith family (owners of Tide-Rider). Both were 18 inch (45.5cm) musical bears, and they were limited to 250 each.

Mr Biddle Mohair and Mr Biddle Plush, on the other hand, were two special bears created to help raise funds for The Gift of Life Foundation, which brings children from various countries to the United States for life-saving heart surgery. The 12 inch (30.5cm) mohair bear was made from a long-pile, tipped fabric, with a black felt waistcoat, while the 15 inch (38cm) plush version was in a more conventional bearish shade, with a waistcoat made from a plaid cloth. In both cases, the Gift of Life logo was added to the waistcoat, and each bear was limited to 250.

The following year, another Gift of Life bear – this time a Cheeky Nurse – appeared in an edition of 250, and the Signature Series was expanded with the addition of Blue Peter and the Bell Boy. The 8 inch (20.5cm) Blue Peter, with only his arms jointed, was a smaller version of the Peter Bear that was first seen in 1962; he was signed by Oliver Holmes. The Bell Boy was of a similar size and was also based on an earlier Merrythought bear, believed to have been made in 1942. Unjointed, he was given a royal blue and black jacket, made from felt, and red velveteen trousers, and was signed by Jacqueline Revitt. Both bears were boxed, and limited to 250 each.

There were also three more Micro Cheekys in editions of that same size. They included a suitably attired Cheeky Little Elf, as well as a Cheeky Little Snowball,

The Micro-sized Cheeky Little Elf was made exclusively for collectors in the USA in 2001.

with a specially rounded body, and an equally rotund Cheeky Little Pumpkin, with his body given the appearance of a Halloween-style lantern.

More recent designs for Tide-Rider have included a number of patriotic Cheekys that followed the events of September 11. The Cheeky Stars & Stripes (8

inches/20.5cm) wore a waistcoat and hat that were decorated with the USA's Stars & Stripes; he was limited to 250. The two Cheeky Allies were similar in size – one wearing Stars & Stripes ribbon and with the American flag embroidered on his foot, and the other wearing a Union Jack ribbon, and with the British flag embroidered on his foot. They were sold as a set, which was limited to 100.

Cheeky "A Hero's Tribute", on the other hand, was a set of three Micro Cheekys, each dressed in the coat and hat of an American fireman, and in the process of raising an American flag. All the bears were made from mohair, and the set was limited to just 50. Like all the Tide-Rider editions, it was exclusive to the U.S.A.

Planes, trains and automobiles were set to be the theme of a new range of Micro Cheekys for 2003, which was also due to see a delightful range of four Cheeky Tea Bears, each representing a different kind of tea. Also planned was a Cheeky sitting in his own Cheeky-decorated teapot.

Other American exclusives have been made for individual shops, and each year a one-of-a-kind auction piece along with a small limited edition is made for the annual teddy bear convention held at Walt Disney World in Florida.

In 1997, for example, the Merrythought pieces went under the title "Come On Pooh, I'll Help You Get to the Convention". The auction bear, known as Bertie, measured a hefty 26 inches (66cm) and was made from a toffee-coloured mohair. He had padded pugs on his paws, and air brushed detailing. On his back was a 12 inch (30.5cm) Winnie-the-Pooh backpack, with a zipped pocket. The limited-edition version consisted of a 12-inch Bertie (30.5cm) and a 6 inch (15cm) Pooh, with a total of just 50 made.

The following year there was a nautical theme, with the auction piece in the form of a 26 inch (66cm) blue Cheeky named Magic, wearing a captain's hat, along with a blue and turquoise collar. The 50 limited-edition bears were blue Micro Cheekys, again in captain's hats and collars.

There were Magical Millennium Cheekys for 1999, and more Cheekys (under the name Cheeky Love and Understanding) for 2000 – when the auction piece measured all of 32 inches (81cm). Jackets were added to

The one-of-a-kind Magical Millennium Cheeky, made for the Disney convention in 1999, was created from a burnished gold mohair, with amethyst-coloured pads in pure silk.

the Cheeky 2001 designs, and a year later Cheeky was back again, but this time masquerading as Winnie-the-Pooh - complete with a Pooh bear suit in gold mohair, and a jacket in bright red felt.

The USA is not the only country for which exclusive Merrythought bears have been produced, however. The firm's distributors in other countries have also ordered many special editions, knowing that collectors love to buy something that is available nowhere else.

In Japan, the firm's distributor is Canal Co. Ltd, which began commissioning exclusive designs for collectors in 1997. Many have been Cheekys, which have been especially popular with Japanese enthusiasts.

The first three were beanbag designs, each measuring 10 inches (25.5cm) and named after flowers and nuts that are common in the Japanese countryside. The brown Cheeky Dongri (Acorn), the yellow Cheeky Tanpopo (Dandelion) and the beige Cheeky Kurumi (Walnut) were each limited to 350.

They were followed two months later by four dressed Cheekys, each 8 inches (20.5cm) in height and in

editions of just 150. Traditional costumes were used for two of them - a beige Ninja Cheeky and the white Happi Cheeky (in the costume associated with the Happi festivals). The other two - Aka Oni Cheeky (red) and Ao Oni Cheeky (blue) - are characters in Japanese fairytales, with devilish horns and tiger print trousers.

In the autumn of 1998, an unlimited Mischief Bride and Groom set was also launched, consisting of special versions of the 8 inch (20.5cm) Master and Miss Mischief, dressed in wedding finery. And there were some further Cheekys that year, including a two-tone version in two sizes (15 and 6 inches/38 and 15cm), made from old

Two-tone Cheekys were created in two sizes for Merrythought's Japanese Distributor, Canal Co., in 1998.

gold mohair with black ears and black pads. A 10 inch (25.5cm) Cheeky from England, on the other hand, was created from a rich green mohair and had a Union Jack on his right pad.

There were three further beanbag Cheekys as well - again measuring 10 inches (25.5cm) but this time limited to 500 each. The pink Sakura, or Cherry Blossom, was named after something widely associated with Japan, while the white Shinju, or Pearl, celebrates the high quality pearls originating in the country. The light blue

A Cheeky and Humpty Dumpty set, made for Japan in 1998, featured a bright green Cheeky with yellow pads.

Marimo (or Aegagropila) was inspired by a type of algae that is found in lakes in the northern part of the country.

By the spring of 1999 there were still more new lines – this time a Cheeky and Humpty Dumpty set, featuring a green 10 inch (25.5cm) Cheeky, and also a pink Cheeky of the same size with a 6 inch (15cm) Cheeky backpack. Both were limited to 300. They were followed in the summer by two 8 inch (20.5cm) Cheekys - the lilac-coloured Cheeky Plum Sherbert and the yellow Cheeky Lemon Sherbert - again limited to 300 each. There was a 10 inch (25.5cm) Cheeky Honey Bee as well. Made from gold mohair and complete with antennae and honey pot, he was in a larger edition of 500.

The following autumn saw yet more beanbag Cheekys, in the same size as the earlier series and in editions of 500 each. Momiji (or coloured maple) was largely yellow, while Koume (Japanese apricot) was mainly pink and Ajisai (hydrangea) blue. There were also two Christmas Cheekys, namely the bright red Cheeky

A delicate pink shade was chosen for a Cheeky carrying a white Cheeky backpack, which was made for Japanese collectors in 1998.

The 10 inch (25.5cm) Cheeky Honey Bee was a Japanese exclusive that appeared in the summer of 1999.

Last Xmas, playing a tune made famous by Wham, and Cheeky Riding Hood, a beige bear in a red cloak. Both had the year (1999) and the words "Making Wishes Come True" embroidered on the left foot.

By the following year, there was a 12 inch (30.cm) Cheeky golly, known as Cheeky Mr Black, in an edition of 750, as well as a 10 inch (25.5cm) Cheeky and Hobby Horse, limited to 500, and a pink Cheeky of the same size holding a white Cheeky puppet (again limited to 500). Another Cheeky, measuring 8 inches (20.5cm) and with the year 2000 embroidered on it, was known as the Millennium Baby and was in a much larger edition of 2,000, while two further Cheekys of that size and made from pure white mohair were dressed as a bride and groom for a Millennium Wedding. In this case, the number of sets was limited to just 200.

Different again was the 8 inch (20.5cm) Cheeky Panda, limited to 300, and with a bell in the middle of his red spotted bow in addition to the familiar bells in his ears. A brightly coloured Punkinhead Chick was the same size, but made from yellow and white mohair with green shorts, red pads and a pink topknot, and with his own "zip-up" egg pouch. He was in an edition of 500. Other new arrivals in that year included Pumpkinhead (an Ancestor of Cheeky with a pumpkin on his head) and a Christmas Cheeky Santa wearing a hooded cloak.

The first arrivals for 2001 were two new Punkinheads – namely a Vintage Punkinhead, replicating a bear in *The Magic of Merrythought* book and the "J.A.P." Punkinhead. This was named after Merrythought Director John Parkes, and was based on a Punkinhead spotted on his desk by visitors from Canal Co.

Cheeky Last Xmas was a musical bear, made for Japan in 1999.

The first ANA bear, made for All Nipon Airways, had a scarf identical to those worn by the airline's stewardesses.

They were soon followed by the multicoloured Punkinhead Fruit Sorbet and Cheeky Fruit Cake (the latter with each paw pad in a different shade). There were also two Cheekys in bunny suits – Cheeky Bunny Tanopo and Cheeky Bunny Sakura. Subsequent editions have included two open-mouthed clowns (known as Punkinhead Looney Circus and Cheeky Loony Circus), and a Cheeky Snowman in hat and scarf, as well as snap-apart Punkinheads with removable limbs (available in red, white or blue) and a Coronation Ancestor of Cheeky combining all three of these colours.

Other designs have been produced for various Japanese stores. They have included a Cheeky Blue Eyes and a Cheeky Orange Eyes (both measuring 10 inches/25.5cm) for the Odakyu department store in Tokyo, as well as various colourful creations (such as Cheeky Carrot Juice) for the Mitsukoshi department store. A Punkinhead Hundred Roses, made from rose pink mohair and with rose-embroidered paws, was a limited edition of 1,000 for the Nagoya Takashimaya department store.

There have also been special bears available only to passengers travelling with All Nipon Airways – the first of

them wearing the same scarf as the airline's stewardesses. In addition, Canal Co. has had a wide range of Merrythought-related items produced under licence – among them figurines of many Merrythought bears as well as everything from clocks and bookends to pens, keychains, handkerchiefs and hand towels decorated with Cheekys and other popular Merrythought teds.

Hong Kong's Animal Kingdom is another distributor that has commissioned various exclusives for sale in the regions in which it operates – starting with three Cheekys to mark the Chinese taking over of Hong Kong in 1997. All had sewn-in uniforms made from green mohair. A set of two other Micro Cheekys – one in red, white and blue and the other with a gold head, red body, and a gold star on its foot (inspired by the Chinese flag) – also marked this event. Given the title Together in Harmony it represented the hope that the friendship between Britain and China would last forever.

Three other Micro Cheekys were also made for the Animal Kingdom in 1997 – a Karate Cheeky and a Budda Cheeky, suitably dressed, and a Ying-Yang Cheeky to depict the Asian philosophy of harmony. The following year there was a further set, inspired by the four seasons,

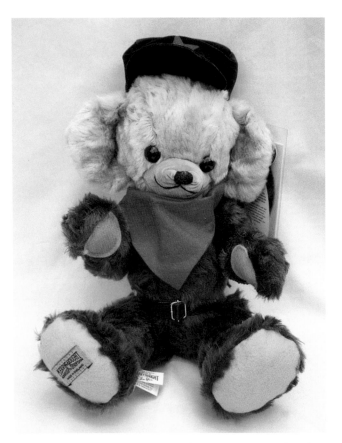

ABOVE: *Cheekys in three sizes were made to commemorate the taking over of Hong Kong by China in 1997.*

TOP RIGHT: *A Micro-sized Budda Cheeky was made for Merrythought's distributor in Hong Kong in 1997.*

BOTTOM RIGHT: *A Tiger Punkinhead was made for Animal Kingdom in Hong Kong in 1998, to celebrate the start of the Chinese Year of the Tiger.*

as well as three 8 inch (20.5cm) bears – a blue Cheeky sold with a golly of the same size; a bean-filled Cheeky; and a Punkinhead Cheeky in a red coat. The latter sold out in two months and was quickly followed by a new 10 inch (25.5cm) Tiger Punkinhead, dressed in a tiger print outfit to celebrate the Chinese Year of the Tiger.

Another Punkinhead, known as Chek Lap Kok and wearing a pilot's goggles and white silk scarf, marked the opening of Hong Kong's new airport that year, and was limited to a mere 50 pieces. They were signed by Merrythought's Oliver Holmes at the launch event in Hong Kong.

The following year there was a Bunny Punkinhead to celebrate the Chinese new year, while a King Tak Chuen Punkinhead stood inside a handmade vase from China's

Out and About Winnie-the-Pooh was made for Debra International in Canada in a limited edition of 1926. © Disney

King Tak Chuen – a place famous for its porcelain. A Chef, a Fisherman, a Kung-Fu Cheeky and a Rider Cheeky were four new Micro Cheekys, and there was a special Millennium Bear – classic in style but made from a pastel pink mohair.

The success of the original 10 inch (25.5cm) Chek Lap Kok and of the Bunny Punkinheads led to the introduction of further sizes later in 1999 – among them giant 26 inch (66cm) examples in editions of just 50. They were followed by a festive Santa Cheeky and a Panda Cheeky, with the latter celebrating the arrival in Hong Kong's Ocean Park of two pandas from mainland China. Both bears were in a 10 inch (25.5cm) size.

Another Bunny Punkinhead, this time in blue, arrived in the year 2000, along with a Dragon Punkinhead, to mark the Year of the Dragon. Both were again initially available only in a 10 inch (25.5cm) size, but additional ones (including a 26 inch/66cm Dragon Punkinhead) followed later in the year. There was a Snowman

Punkinhead, too, and a Micro version of the Pilot Punkinhead. Then, early in 2001, they were joined by a Green Bunny Punkinhead as well as a Snake Punkinhead – the latest in the line of Chinese Zodiac animals.

Two characters from a traditional Chinese fairytale – the Monkey God Songoku and the Pig God Tyohakkai – also appeared in Punkinhead form that year, followed by the monk Sanzou and his white horse early in 2002. Other 21st century designs have included an Emperor Punkinhead and a Great Wall Punkinhead (with the words Great Wall on his left foot) and a World Cup Soccer Punkinhead in the same 10 inch (25.5cm) size, with black pads and topknot and emblazoned with a black and white football. A Terracotta Punkinhead followed, along with a Micro version of the Great Wall Punkinhead.

Other designs have been commissioned by Animal Kingdom for individual stores – not just in Hong Kong but in Canada as well – and a number of special editions

181

Cheeky Down Under was the first Merrythought to be produced specially for Australian collectors, and appeared in November 1998.

were also commissioned by Merrythought's previous distributor in Canada, Debra International. Early examples of these included a lavender-tipped Micro Cheeky and a jet black one. But an even more dramatic offering was the exclusive Out and About Winnie-the-Pooh, which was limited to 1926 – the year in which the first of the Pooh books was published. The special version of the famous bear was housed in a copy of an old steamship trunk, and came with his own passport and other travelling essentials, including a small honey pot.

A Where it all Began Pooh followed, featuring an 8 inch (20.5cm) Pooh. He was sitting in a 14 inch (35.5cm) replica of a monument in White River, Ontario, where a real bear cub named Winnie originated. This cub was donated to London Zoo – and went on to provide Winnie-the-Pooh with part of his name.

In 1999, Debra International commissioned a 10 inch (25.5cm) Frosted Maple Cheeky in a silky, off-white mohair, with a red maple leaf embroidered on his left foot. Later, the Millennium was marked with a pink and white Punkinhead wearing purple shorts on which a silver maple leaf and the year 2000 had been embroidered. Other designs for Canada included an Ancestor of Cheeky Clown that was given a pink costume, trimmed with yellow, along with a yellow and black clown's hat perched on his topknot.

In November 1998, an Australian exclusive, Cheeky Down Under, was also launched, wearing a drover's style waterproof jacket and a hat made from waxed cotton. It was the first ever Merrythought to be made for sale only in the Australian market.

Other exclusives have been produced for sale in countries closer to home. Some of the earliest were

This Ironbridge-type bear was made from an old Dyson Hall fabric for a bear week held in The Netherlands.

commissioned by Van Gorcum Teddyberen Benelux, Merrythought's distributor in the Netherlands, Belgium and Luxembourg. As far back as 1991, the firm was selling a dusky blue version of the Ironbridge Bear, made from old Dyson Hall mohair that had been found at the Merrythought factory. He was limited to just 79, since that was all that could be made from the available cloth. The bear carried a red rosette which indicated that he was made for the third bear week to be held in the Dutch town of Gorinchem (or Gorcum).

Among the other designs made for Van Gorcum was a Netherlands Bear, wearing a blue and white Dutch scarf and produced specially for the eighth Dutch bear festival, at Amerongen Castle, in 1996. Measuring 7.5 inches (19cm), he was limited to just 48. A later event at

the same venue was commemorated by a bear in a traditional Dutch striped waistcoat and limited to just 12.

Totally different again was the Cheeky Viking, complete with helmet and shield, which was made for Scandinavian distributor Margarethas Dockskap in Malmo, Sweden. A more traditional bear, Sean, was produced for Irish Creative Ltd in Co. Kildare. Made from an unusual, rich green mohair, he wore a printed waistcoat decorated with shamrocks, and his footpads were made from the same fabric.

The colours of the Irish flag were used in the making of Patrick, a limited edition of 500 for Ireland's T.E.L., in 1998.

The Cheeky Viking was made for Merrythought's Scandinavian distributor.

Ireland's Teddy Exclusives (T.E.L.), on the other hand, have commissioned a number of striking Cheekys, starting in 1998 with Patrick, who was produced in the colours of the Irish flag. Measuring 15 inches (38cm), and limited to just 500, his head, body and limbs were in a bright green mohair, while bright orange was used for his snout, and his pads were pure white. A sprig of shamrock was attached to his paw. In due course, a Patrick Junior, measuring just 8 inches (20.5cm) and limited to 250, was also introduced.

By then there had also been a cuddly Squeaky Cheeky, measuring 17.5 inches (44.5cm) and made from cream and fawn mohair, with an unusually soft filling. He had a squeaker in his body, and was limited to just 250. An 8 inch (20.5cm) version, in an edition of the same size, later followed.

Different again was the multi-coloured Rainbow Cheeky – in the same size as the original Squeaky but later followed by a Micro version. And then there were some Cheeky Little Leprechauns, each complete with an uncirculated one punt Irish coin contained in a small money pouch.

Other designs are appearing all the time, and are sometimes described in the International Collectors' Club magazine, so that enthusiasts in other countries can recognize them as well.

The multi-coloured Rainbow Cheeky was one of several Cheekys made exclusively for T.E.L. in Ireland.

Chapter 13

13. THE MERRYTHOUGHT INTERNATIONAL COLLECTORS' CLUB

In 1995, to the delight of enthusiasts, Merrythought launched its International Collectors' Club – with benefits that included new opportunities to acquire special Merrythought bears. Every year there would be an exclusive bear, available only to club members, and the annual club Open Days also led to the design of many more unusual and interesting creations – ranging from one-offs for the Silent Auctions to inexpensive cuddly teddies for those with smaller budgets.

The first club magazine, in the autumn of 1995, introduced the 1995/1996 Limited Edition Club Bear, known as Hampton. Inspired by the magnificent Hampton Court, the 15 inch (38cm) bear was made from a glowing russet mohair, with paw pads of peach-coloured raw silk –

Hampton

Windsor

Blenheim

Chatsworth

A Limited Edition Club Bear is produced each year, available only to members.

Hampton 1995-6
Blenheim 1996-7
Chatsworth 1997-8
Warwick 1998-9
Windsor 1999-2000
Buckingham 2000-2001
Caernafon 2001-2002
Glamis 2002-2003

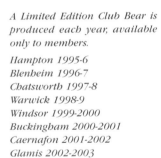

Buckingham

Warwick

Glamis

Caernafon

187

shades reminiscent of those seen in the beautiful Tudor brick building. Round his neck was a cravat featuring the club's emblem, which also appeared on his right foot.

The stately homes theme was continued the following year with the introduction of Blenheim, inspired by the palace built for the first Duke of Marlborough. This time, the mohair used was a luxurious stone-coloured one, and the bear's features included shaving around the mouth, to give him a whiskered look, as well as thumbs on the front paws. A waistcoat made from Chinese brocade in royal blue and gold completed the look.

Chatsworth - named after the country house - became the third Limited Edition Club Bear, available only during the year 1997/1998. His mohair was the colour of Derbyshire stone, and he wore a smart bow tie made from a creamy chintz.

A year later there was Warwick, who took his name from the medieval castle. Made from a sumptuous mohair tipped in a burnished copper shade, he had pads in a green and blue patterned brocade, and a matching Tudor-style cap from the same material.

Then there was Windsor, whose long, textured mohair was an antique gold shade. Since the castle after which he was named is famous for its Norman Tower, designer Jacqueline Revitt gave the bear a Norman-style collar made from a red and black brocade that was overlaid with black and gold strap work.

Buckingham the following year took his name from the palace - originally known as Buckingham House but sold to the Crown during the reign of King George III. Since no Georgian could consider himself a gentleman without a luxurious brocade waistcoat, the bear was given one as well - created from a beautiful, oriental brocade with a silk back and lining. The bear himself had curly blond mohair, with brown ultrasuede pads.

The noble bear for 2001/2002 had as his namesake the Welsh castle Caernafon, and was in a honey gold, tufted mohair with matching velveteen pads. An ivy green tie made from shot satin and embroidered with the Prince of Wales plumes provided the finishing touch.

He was followed by Glamis - that being the Scottish castle that was the childhood home of Queen Elizabeth the Queen Mother, and where Princess Margaret was born in the same year that Merrythought was established (1930). A silvery grey mohair was chosen for the bear's fur,

and he was given a traditional plaid sash set off by a spray of heather.

Each of these Collectors' Club exclusives was available for a full year, and recently there have also been a couple of other designs available only to club members. In 2001, for example, the first members only Annual Christmas Teddy Bear was introduced, wearing a striking red cape embroidered with holly motifs and the year; he was limited to just 250. A few months later, the pure white Valentine followed - with bright red pads and holding a red, heart-shaped cushion on which a special message could be embroidered.

Other bears produced for club members have been on sale only at the annual Open Days organised for the club each July. The designs have included a special Open Day Commemorative Bear each year - initially only available to those members who were able to attend the event, held in and around the Ironbridge factory.

The first, in 1996, was Strawberry Tea, who was in the process of brushing away the last of the picnic crumbs with a cotton napkin in a wild strawberry print. (A larger, one-of-a-kind version was also made as the prize in a special entrance ticket draw - a custom repeated in the following years.) A year later there was Toffee Apple, in a toffee-coloured mohair with a cheerful red gingham bow, and carrying his own toffee apple. Then in 1998 came Lemon Sorbet, made from lemon-coloured mohair with a lemon cotton print bow round her head, and sitting in her own, stencilled lemon crate.

A year later, Picnic Bear was the chosen design. She had a bean-filled tummy, feet and paws, and came with her own raffia hamper, complete with cotton tartan tablecloth and napkin. Then in 2000 came the last of the Picnic in the Park Series - this time a Celebration Bear (marking the club's fifth anniversary), made from a rich Butterscotch mohair with a printed, quilted bow tie, and sitting in his own wicker wine cradle.

The following year, 2001, saw the start of a brand-new Woodland series, beginning with Willow - made from scrunched golden mohair and sitting, fittingly, in a hand-woven willow basket. The basket was lined with a handkerchief made from the same print fabric as the muffler round the bear's neck. Poppy followed in 2002, carrying her own little posy and complete with a gardener's trug. Both these bears in the Woodland Flowers and Foliage series were also available by mail order to those unable to attend the event.

Those who have been able to make it to Ironbridge, however, have had the chance to pick up a whole range of other exclusive bears. Always in demand are the Artist Proof Edition Bears, for example – each one in a small limited edition, and produced initially without nose or ribbon. Collectors can choose their own style and colour of nose stitching and their own ribbon, to give them a bear that is totally unique.

In 1997 there were no fewer than 22 designs, ranging from the saggy Bertie and Billy to the "pretty in pink" Candyfloss, and from the traditional little 6 inch (15cm) ted by the name of Murphy to the giant Bigheart – a hefty 28 inches (71cm) and standing on all fours. Some of the editions were exceptionally small – there were only two Bighearts, for example.

Choc Chip was one of the Artist Proof Editions in 2000.

Jake was one of the Artist Proof Edition Bears made for the first Open Day in 1996.

Among the designs in 1998 were the musical Mr Melody and the Yes/No Chocolate Orange (who took his name from his unusual tipped mohair), while the Yes/No Blackie on all fours and various bears in striking colours were among those on offer in 1999. A year later, the choice included three Cheekys – two in pastel shades and a third in a tipped mohair – and there have been others in the years since then, as well as more traditional designs in a huge range of colours.

The idea proved so popular that, in 1999, Merrythought went a stage further and offered a limited number of personalized Kit Bears. These were only partially stitched and could be completed by club members, under the guidance of Merrythought staff (who would also be happy to take over should the bear's owner prefer it). Available in a range of colours, they could be stuffed and finished entirely to the new owner's own specifications.

A year later, they were followed by an Embroidered Bear, again available in a choice of mohairs. The foot pads could be embroidered with the owner's initials or a short name, or a date if preferred, to make them totally unique.

In 2001, enthusiasts were offered something even more special. This time the Kit Bear was a fully jointed one, available in various jewel-coloured mohairs. Collectors could choose their own form of stuffing, their own eye colours, and their preferred style of nose, and then follow their new acquisition as it progressed through

Special bears can be won in the various games and competitions; this one was the star prize in the 1996 Bearbola.

Commemorative Bear made from an interesting plush, and a variety of other inexpensive teds have also been made for the events. Others are sometimes given away as prizes in the various games and competitions that add an enjoyable extra dimension to the day's fun each year. It is, however, impossible to itemize every single design here; as with so many of the special bears, many of them are not even detailed in the Merrythought archives (especially if they simply involve the combining of an existing pattern with a new kind of plush). No doubt, in years to come, these will become as much of a mystery to collectors as some of the early specials and exclusives are today.

Each year, the bears made specially for the Open Day include inexpensive examples for those with smaller budgets; this one was on sale in 2001.

the factory, being made up to their own specifications. Special embroidery on the footpad and their own choice of ribbon provided the finishing touches. A totally different design was available a year later, and a limited number of the made-up bears were also available to members unable to attend the event.

All club members can also place bids for the one-of-a-kind bears in the annual Silent Auctions. These are among the most coveted of all the Open Day designs and, like the Artist Proof Editions, they have included a wide variety of sizes and designs, to suit every imaginable taste. Giant Cheekys and Punkinheads in magnificent mohairs always attract a great deal of interest, but there are also traditional bears in unusual and beautiful mohairs, as well as totally out-of-the-ordinary characters – some based on designs from days gone by and others totally original.

Those with smaller budgets are not forgotten either, however. Each year there is a special, unjointed,

Chapter 14

14. LABELS

Merrythought has used a number of different labels on its bears – often on one of the foot pads. Old labels were occasionally used, however, so they do not guarantee that a bear was made at a particular time.

A celluloid-covered metal button, with the Merrythought wishbone trademark and including the words Hygienic Merrythought Toys, was used for a while in the 1930s. Usually it was fixed to the ear of the bear, but sometimes (especially in the case of smaller examples) it was placed on the back or shoulder. Merrythought is an old English word meaning wishbone.

Woven labels were used in the 1930s, and are also seen on some post-war examples.

A wider woven label was used for a time in the mid 1950s; examples are rare.

Printed labels were introduced after the Second World War; this type was first used around the late 1950s.

A white printed label with the words "REGD DESIGN" added was used on some post-war toys until the 1960s. A printed label with a white, woven "REGD DESIGN" strip was also used.

In the 1980s, a new type of printed label was introduced, with the yellow colour painted on, rather than woven into the cloth as before. It was a stronger colour than that used earlier, but tended to rub off.

New woven labels were introduced in 1991.

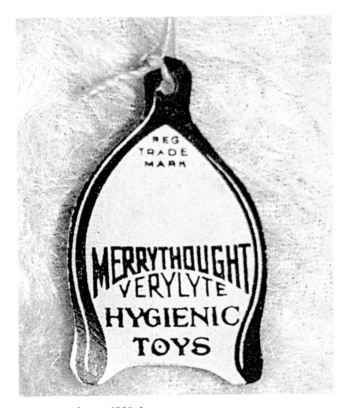

A swing tag from a 1930s bear.

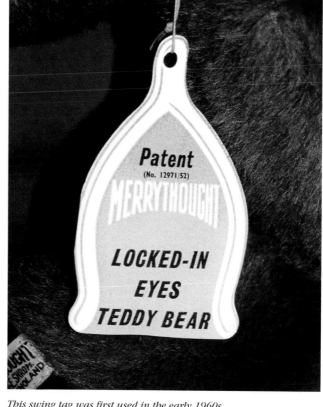

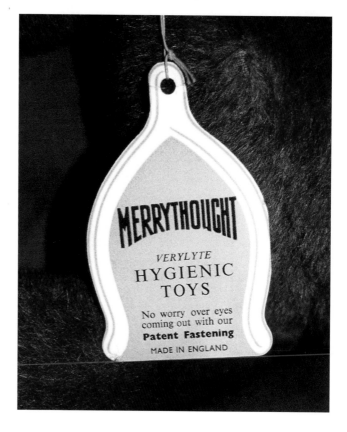

ABOVE AND BELOW: *Swing tags of this type were used in the late 1950s.*

This swing tag was first used in the early 1960s.

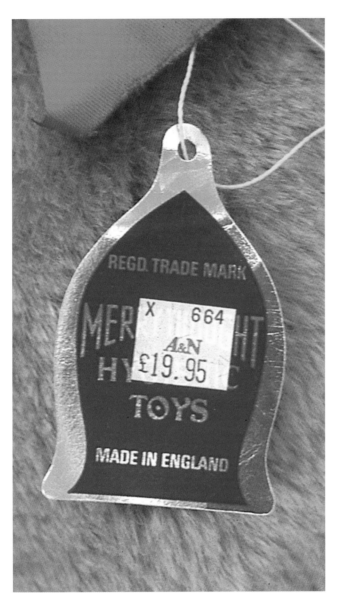

A swing tag on a 1980s bear.

A new swing tag was introduced in the mid 1980s.

INDEX